The Parables of Jesus

OTHER BOOKS BY FATHER FILAS

The Man Nearest to Christ
The Family for Families
Joseph and Jesus
Joseph Most Just
His Heart in Our Work (ed.)

The
PARABLES of JESUS

A Popular Explanation
by

FRANCIS L. FILAS, S. J.

NEW YORK   THE MACMILLAN COMPANY   1959

IMPRIMI POTEST: *William J. Schmidt, S.J.*
Provincial, Chicago Province, Society of Jesus
June 16, 1958

NIHIL OBSTAT: *Austin G. Schmidt, S.J.*
Censor Librorum
July 2, 1958

IMPRIMATUR: *Rt. Rev. Msgr. George J. Casey*
Administrator, Archdiocese of Chicago
July 3, 1958

© *FRANCIS L. FILAS 1959*

First Printing

Library of Congress catalog card number: 59-5767

The Macmillan Company, New York
Macmillan-Brett Ltd., Galt, Ontario

Printed in the United States of America

The Purpose of This Book

If there is one thing certain about this book, it is the fact that it is not exploring a new field. Dozens of scholarly works have been written upon the subject. The treatment in many of them is surprisingly similar, and the reasons behind an approach practically so identical must be the difficulties which all these authors have encountered—for the parables of Jesus *are* often enough quite difficult.

On their surface many of them present a deceptive appearance of simplicity, as if the mind of a child could plumb them to their depths at once. It is only upon further and more careful reading that one notices surface obscurities, contrasts, paradoxes, unexpected conclusions. Yet we know that these stories came from the infallibly wise mind of our Lord, animated by a love in His Sacred Heart that wished all men to learn of Him and come to Him. Jesus had His reasons for teaching so much in parables. We must patiently search out the answers to our question, "Why?"

This book was written with one purpose in mind: to condense and summarize the commonly accepted interpretations of our Lord's parables so as to make them easily accessible to the reader unskilled in biblical lore. Discussion groups and study clubs can use it as a nucleus for further comment. It does not intend to lay down absolutely apodictic doctrines, for the interpretations in each case depend on each case. None the less, it will have reached its goal if it reveals some of the treasures of meaning which Jesus put into His words.

"Out of the abundance of the heart the mouth speaks"—there remains the pleasant task of formally dedicating the efforts of this book to Jesus, Mary, and Joseph, in deepest thanksgiving.

FRANCIS L. FILAS, S.J., S.T.D.

Loyola University
Chicago, Illinois
Feast of St. Thomas Aquinas, 1958

Table of Contents

The Parables of Jesus

What Are the Parables of Jesus?

One possible source of confusion can be removed at once if we understand what is meant by the parables of Jesus. There are parables in a strict sense of the word, and parables in a wide sense that are condensed into proverbial phrases or sayings. In this book we intend to speak of all of these, no matter how they might be rigidly classified. The reason is that even the short parabolic sayings sometimes need detailed explanation much more than the lengthy parables themselves.

The purpose behind the parable can be obscured if we stay with the strict meaning of our English word as it is derived from the Greek. It gives us clues and the main outlines of the idea, but it does not yet fulfill the concept of the Hebrew parable as Jesus used it.

"Parable" is derived from the Greek *parabolē*, appearing in Latin as *parabola*. Its root meaning is from the combination of *para*—"beside"—and *ballein*—"to throw." It means, then, a placing beside or a comparison. Since this comparison would be done by means of speech, the idea of *speaking* moved through Italian and French to appear in English as "parole" (one's word), "parlance" (one's manner of speech), or even "parlor" (the speaking room). However, the idea of *comparison* stayed with our word "parable" as we use it today.

We have many figures of speech in which comparisons appear, but we do not call all of them parables. Thus, a *metaphor* contains a comparison but is not expressed as such, as, for example, a "frowning cliff" or a "raging sea." A *simile* occurs when a comparison is expressed, as, "a cliff has a beetling brow like a man who is frowning." When the *metaphor* is *extended* so that practically every detail teaches some truth by its comparison, we call this an *allegory*. Such would be our Lord's allegory, "I am the Good Shepherd, and I know My own, and My own know Me, as the Father knows Me, and I know the Father; and I lay down My life for My sheep" (Jn. 10:14–15). When the *simile* becomes *extended*, we have the case of the parable in the strict sense of the word. "The Kingdom of Heaven is like a grain of mustard" (Mt. 13:31).

The parable was intended to express a lesson of wisdom. Hence, it was described by the Hebrew term *mashal*, which indicates a short saying of profound meaning. Under this heading we should place the proverb and allegory as well as the strict parable, for this wider sense seems to be the one followed in the gospels. This is an important point to note. The parables of Jesus can be pure parable, pure allegory, or a mixture of the two that does not follow strict laws of comparison but is intent only on teaching a supernatural lesson.

Various definitions of the parable can be given: "a developed comparison or extended simile teaching and illustrating a supernatural truth"; "a story of some actual or possible happening, drawn from nature, to exemplify a supernatural fact"; or "a literary device used to illustrate a moral and religious truth by means of an imaginary but entirely plausible fact." Yet again we must emphasize that the Hebrew parable, as Jesus used it to perfection, is not obliged to follow the laws of an airtight definition. In interpreting our Lord's words the following principles should be kept in mind:

1. Since the parable is a developed comparison, its principal

lesson is to be found by presenting the narrative in the two terms of its comparison.

2. Secondary details are to be recognized as such, and must be subordinated to the principal lesson. On the one hand they should not be given such emphasis that they are thought to be the heart of the parable; but on the other hand they should not be so neglected as to lose their reinforcement of the principal lesson, or perhaps their teaching of a lesson of their own. How does one find these secondary details? Usually, they are contained in the first part of the parable, which is the image or illustration. They will not, however, appear in the second part, which is the application or the lesson.

3. We should also note the existence of literary details which have the purpose of making the story sound more natural and easy flowing, but which in themselves could be dropped without harming the imagery or the lesson of the parable.

4. In general, the parables of Jesus will describe the course of nature in some way or other, but they are not obliged to follow everyday reality down to the last detail. Many times they will do so, but if it suits the teaching purpose of their creator to invent a fictitious background no one can justly accuse the teacher of deception. Jesus never claimed that His illustrations had to be actual history.

5. Some parables end with an "apparent" conclusion which should not be interpreted as part of their main lesson. The first illustration and the logical lesson should certainly be accepted; but suppose that, added to this, there appears a maxim or proverb like "The last shall be first and the first last," or "Many are called, but few are chosen" (cf. Mt. 20:16; 22:14). In such a case it would seem that this final sentence should not be forced to fit within the parable itself; and, vice versa, the lesson of the parable should not be forced to fit the final maxim. These closing words will then serve as a further reflection, but not necessarily, we repeat, as the lesson of the parable.

The "Kingdom of Heaven"

One of the most puzzling expressions in the parables of Jesus is His use of the phrase "Kingdom of Heaven." It is puzzling, that is, to readers who do not know what it meant to Jesus and to His countrymen. Taken in the background of contemporary Jewish customs and ways of speaking, it can become reasonably clear even to us who are removed from Jesus' homeland and times by thousands of miles and many centuries.

The first thing to notice is that Matthew's gospel regularly uses the term "Kingdom of Heaven" where Luke and Mark employ "Kingdom of God." Both phrases mean the same thing, but since Matthew was writing for a predominantly Jewish audience, he adapted himself to the Jewish custom of reverent reticence in the use of the name of God. This reverence led to the substitution of circumlocutions or other titles of God in order to avoid pronouncing the august name.

Luke and Mark wrote for gentile converts interested in or already members of Christianity. Hence, they expressed Jesus' idea in terms which their readers could understand: "Kingdom of God." The words which Jesus Himself originally used must have been "Kingdom of Heaven," since He logically accommodated Himself to the religious customs of His time.

This explanation removes at its root the confusion of the modern

Christian who hears the parables from the pulpit and reads them in his missal, wondering all the time how "Kingdom of Heaven" can be understood in terms of the "Heaven" that is the place of eternal happiness with God. How, indeed, can the "Kingdom of Heaven" in this sense grow like a mustard seed? Or contain good and bad fishes which will be sorted out in the end? Or grow both genuine wheat mixed with counterfeit weed? The answer is simple. If we still wish to interpret "Heaven" in this sense of eternal reward, we can always think of the spiritual kingdom on earth that *prepares* for Heaven. This is truly the kingdom of God—first, militantly fighting the battle against evil and the powers of darkness, and then ultimately by God's grace triumphing in the attainment of eternal joy. Truly, too, the kingdom of God on earth becomes the kingdom of eternal life in Heaven by anticipation.

Yet we must emphasize that this particular meaning was not at the heart of Christ's words. He was speaking to a people whose religious tradition had been steeped in the fact that they had been chosen by God for a divine mission. Temporarily, so they believed, the power and the glory of ancient Israel had left them, but eventually this power and glory would return. They were correct in looking forward to the Messiah, the Anointed One, as the representative of God who would rule this new kingdom, but their interpretation fell short of its ideal goal when the kingdom of God's power came to be anticipated in a purely earthly sense. They expected a return of military might and political dominion over other nations. Incidentally, the title "Christ" is merely the Greek equivalent of the Hebrew "Anointed One" or Messiah. It signified a king, a priest, and a prophet.

We must keep in mind that Jesus was dealing with a very delicate situation. On the one hand He wished to retain and deepen the already strong tradition of God's forthcoming ambassador. With equal vigor Jesus had to protect His message of the kingdom from a temporal and merely earthly interpretation. Humanly speaking (and setting aside for the moment the possibility of miraculous intervention), our Lord's teaching mission would have been cut short if He had allowed the people to think of Him as a political visionary. The resultant revolt and inevitable suppression by Roman authorities would have hindered Him from promulgating the new law of love before His time of apparent defeat was to come.

Moreover, for the sake of truth itself, it was even more important that Jesus' message be properly understood. He had come on this earth to establish a kingdom, but it was to be a kingdom of deep faith in the word of God, of unshakable hope amid earthly misfortune, and mainly of active love of God and man. The kingdom of God on earth was to exist amid those circumstances in which the will of God would be ideally obeyed. To convey His message in a gentle yet effective manner, Jesus used the deliberately gradual and somewhat obscure method of teaching the nature of the kingdom by means of His parables.

Seen in the light of proper explanation, the parables take on ever more meaning, in proportion as the logic behind them becomes more clear. Yet a truly profound problem remains that has troubled the minds of many for many centuries. Why did Jesus seem to shut out His listeners from the very truth He came to proclaim to them? While apparently blaming them for not receiving His message, did He not say equivalently that in the circumstances they could not have acted otherwise? This is the heart of the difficulty. It is based on a long passage in Matthew, and appears even more strongly in the compressed account of Mark.

And the disciples came and asked Him, "Why dost Thou speak to them in parables?" "Because," He said to them in reply, "it is granted to you to know the mysteries of the Kingdom of Heaven; but to them it is not granted. For whoever possesses, to him more shall be given, and he shall have abundance; while whoever possesses not, even that which he has shall be taken from him. I, therefore, speak to them in parables, because, though seeing, they do not see, and though hearing, they do not listen nor understand. So in their case is fulfilled the prophecy of Isaiah, which says: 'You will listen and listen, and by no means understand; and you will gaze and gaze, and by no means see.

7

For this people's heart is grown gross, and their ears are dull of hearing, and their eyes they have closed; lest ever they should see with their eyes, and hear with their ears, and understand with their heart, and should be converted and I should heal them.' " (Mt. 13:10–15; cf. Isaiah 6:9–10)

Mark presents the same discourse in summary:

And when He had gone aside, those who were about Him with the twelve asked Him the meaning of the parable. "To you," He answered them, "is given the secret of the Kingdom of God; but to the outsiders everything is presented in parables that 'they may gaze and gaze, and not perceive, and may listen and listen, and not understand; lest they should return, and their sins should be forgiven them.' " (Mk. 4:10–12)

Scripture scholars who have commented on this passage have noted that the "outsiders" mentioned here were not locked out of a closed circle, but of their own free will wished to remain strangers to the truth of Christ's doctrine. To those of good will (the disciples, on the "inside") the parables would have the effect of bringing ever more light.

We have already explained that Jesus had to use His parables as a veiled method of gradually and safely teaching the doctrine of His spiritual kingdom. It is unthinkable that our Lord would have wished to teach *in order* to increase the guilt of those in bad will. He had come to teach the truth of a law of love. Why would He speak in order to multiply sin? The most that can be said with regard to the use of parables for malevolent listeners is that the very obscurity of His parabolic language was able to prevent the fullness of knowledge on the part of an evil-minded audience. Such knowledge would have made the cup of their guilt run over by removing all causes for blameless ignorance.

But this is certainly not the whole answer. The "mystery" of the Kingdom of Heaven was something sacred which could be understood more deeply only by those who had the good will and the opportunity to accept further instruction concerning it. Jesus quoted on this score a worldly proverb. Normally, the wealthy by reason of their riches become wealthier, and the poor by reason of their destitution become poorer as their means decrease. The proverb has a spiritual application in this case.

Men and women of good will are spiritually rich, and as they correspond with God's grace they grow in their wealth; but those who are spiritually destitute are poor because of their bad will. It is this fault on their part which contributes to their further falling away from God's service. The proverb as Christ cited it in no way indicates an arbitrary preference for some and a corresponding reprobation of others on God's part, independently of individual merits.

Jesus' quotation from Isaiah is to be understood in its context. Semitic imagery, as used here, is strong and vivid. God as the first cause of all creation is logically pictured as the direct cause of every event. The results of human reaction to God's grace are often described *as if* God had directly intended such results, no matter what were to be the workings of man's free will. In Isaiah's case, God is pictured as speaking with strong irony, to impress on His people that their stubbornness in accepting His law would be the cause of His rejecting them.

Thus, this passage can be understood in the sense that our Lord's words were only the occasion and not the cause for bad will to be manifested. However, the full meaning is apparently something else. It is an emphasis on the value of the parables as a vehicle of doctrine. From the parables people of good will could obtain further enlightenment. Those in bad will could not, as it were, single out any particular detail for condemnation because of the parables' obscurity. By reason of that bad will, too, they would have been looking for some pretext to prevent Christ from exercising His apostolate. Those, however, who were moving toward the light would find food for tantalizing and earnest reflection in the word images Jesus had put into their minds.

In no case was the slightest injustice done to the listeners. The degree of their sincerity was to be the measure of their success in accepting the spiritual nature of Christ's kingdom. Such for us, too, is the ultimate lesson of the parables.

*   *   *

Before proceeding to the explanation of the parables, it is well to call attention to the nature of the accuracy of the gospels. Matthew, Mark, and Luke are called the "synoptic gospels," not because they give a synopsis or summary of our Lord's deeds and words, but because (in the root sense of the Greek *syn*—"with"— and *opsis*—"sight") so many of their accounts parallel one another that they can be placed in columns and compared at a glance. This does not mean that their periodic discrepancies are to be charged to faulty reporting.

The accounts they present were never intended to be exact to the individual word and phrase, agreeing in every detail as if they had been copied by means of a mechanical recorder. Instead, their aim is to be substantially accurate. Each gospel writer has acted as an editor with regard to his material, which was largely oral tradition of the primitive Christian community, faithfully handed down from the first eyewitnesses. Some expressions might have been misunderstood by the particular audience at which his gospel was aimed. These are often softened from an original text seemingly harsh to non-Jewish ears. Again, explanatory phrases and translations are inserted for the benefit of gentile recipients.

It is commonly accepted that Matthew wrote his gospel first in an Aramaic original, of which we have no extant copy. Mark followed, using Matthew as one of his sources as well as the recollections of Peter. Luke then reworked this previous material with the aid of new eyewitnesses and the testimony of Christ's mother Mary and St. Paul. At this point Matthew's Aramaic text was edited and translated into Greek, as we now have it today. These three gospels, then, were completed before A.D. 70, the date of the fall of Jerusalem. The fourth gospel, that of St. John, followed an independent pattern of presenting material concerning Jesus which the first three evangelists had not included.

The Parables

THE SOWER AND HIS SEED

Mt. 13:1-9

On that day Jesus going out of the house sat down by the seaside. And great crowds collected about Him, so that He went into a boat and sat in it, while all the crowd stood on the shore. And He spoke many things to them in parables, saying, "Behold, the sower went out to sow; and as he sowed some seeds fell along the roadside, and the birds came and devoured them. And other seeds fell upon the stony places where they had not much soil; and they sprouted quickly on account of having no depth of soil; but when the sun rose they were scorched, and they withered for want of root. And others fell among the briers; and the briers grew up and choked them. But others fell upon the good soil, and yielded a crop, some a hundredfold, some sixtyfold, and some thirtyfold. He that has ears to hear, let him hear!"

Mt. 13:18-23

"You, therefore, shall hear the meaning of the parable of the sower. When any one hears the Word of the Kingdom, and does not understand it, the Evil One comes and snatches away what has been sown in his heart. This is that sown along the roadside. And that sown upon the stony ground is the one who hears the Word, and accepts it at once with delight; yet he has no root in himself, but is only temporary; and when trouble or persecution arises on account of the Word, he immediately falls away. And that sown among the briers is the one who hears the Word; but the anxieties of this world and the seductions of wealth choke the Word, and it becomes unproductive. But that sown upon good soil is the one who hears and understands the Word, and who really produces fruit; and yields, one a hundredfold, another sixtyfold, and another thirtyfold."

Mk. 4:1–9

And again He began to teach by the seaside. And a vast crowd gathered about Him, so that He got into a boat and sat out on the Sea, while all the crowd were on the land by the waterside. And He taught them many things in parables; and He said to them in the course of His teaching: "Listen! Behold, the sower went out to sow; and as he sowed, some seed fell along the roadside, and the birds came and devoured it. And some fell upon rocky ground where it had not much soil; and it sprang up quickly because of having no depth of soil; and when the sun rose it was scorched, and withered for want of root. And some fell among briers; and the briers grew up and choked it, and it produced no crop. And others fell upon good soil, and yielded a growing and increasing crop, and produced, one thirtyfold, one sixtyfold, and one a hundredfold." And He added, "He that has ears to hear, let him hear!"

Mk. 4:13–20

Then He said to them, "Do you not understand this parable? How then will you understand any parable? The sower sows the Word. And those along the roadside are they in whom the Word is sown; and when they have heard it, Satan immediately comes and takes away the Word which has been sown in them. And those that are sown in rocky places are they, who on hearing the Word, accept it at once with joy; but having no root in themselves, they are only temporary; then, when trouble or persecution arises on account of the Word, they immediately fall away. And those that are sown among the briers are they who hear the Word; but the anxieties of the world, and the seductions of wealth, and inordinate desires for other things enter, and choke the Word, and it becomes unproductive. But those that are sown upon good soil are they that hear the Word and accept it, and produce fruit—one thirty-fold, one sixtyfold, and one a hundredfold."

Lk. 8:4–8

Now when a great crowd was gathering, and people from every town were resorting to Him, He addressed them in a parable: "The sower went out to sow his seed; and as he sowed, some seed fell along the roadside, where it was trodden upon, and the birds of the air devoured it. And some fell upon the rock; but on sprouting, it withered for lack of moisture. And some fell amid the briers, and the briers grew up with it and choked it. And some fell upon good soil; and springing up it yielded a hundredfold crop." As He said this He cried out, "He that has ears to hear, let him hear!"

Lk. 8:11–15

"Now the parable means this: The seed is the Word of God. And those along the roadside are they that have heard; then comes the devil, and takes away the Word from their heart, that they may not believe and be saved. And those upon the rock are they who, when they hear, receive the Word with delight; yet these have no root; they believe for a while, and in the hour of trial fall away. And that falling among the briers are they that have heard; yet, as they go on their way, are choked by the anxieties and riches and pleasures of life, and bring no fruit to maturity. But that upon the good soil are they who, with a noble and generous heart, having heard the Word, hold it fast, and yield fruit with endurance."

The parable of the sower is the most important of Jesus' parables concerning His kingdom. It is a simple story. A farmer in his field scatters seed, and as the seed falls from his hand some of it falls on the roadside, where birds snatch it up; other seed falls on thin soil over rock, where it quickly withers after a short growth; and still other seed grows up amid thistles and thorns, which choke it to death. Finally, the seed falling on good ground brings a return of thirtyfold, sixtyfold, and a hundredfold.

When the disciples later ask Jesus for an explanation of the parable, He describes the Evil One as snatching the word of God out of men's hearts just as the birds have stolen the seed. The seed on stony ground represents the inconstant hearts of fair-weather believers. The briers are the worldly cares which drown out the call of God. The seed on good ground indicates the persevering acceptance of God's word by the true believer.

Certain characteristics of this story are notably parabolic. It does not deal with "a sower," but "the sower," so typical is it to be. Again, it does not enter into judgment on the carelessness of a farmer who would scatter his seed so prodigally and thoughtlessly over unfruitful portions of his field. The parable is also out of touch with actual conditions in its description of a harvest ranging from thirtyfold to the stupendous sixtyfold and hundredfold, all an unbelievably high return for the agricultural conditions of the time.

Commentators have noted that the parallelism between thorns and the interests of the world, between rocky ground and fickle piety seems true to form; but does it seem logical to put the "birds of heaven" into the same category with the devil snatching souls as they snatch seed? And where would the action of the believer's free will be exemplified in seed which is helplessly devoured by the devil, again with no help from the sower?

The answer must be, of course, that the parable is not obliged to use every one of its details in artificially exact fashion. It is interested only in telling its story and drawing its intended lesson.

That lesson must be logically sought in the words of Jesus, for in this instance we have the explanation of the parable from His own lips. The central point of the parable is always the *seed,* and the comparison is to follow the fortunes of the seed alone.

The seed here represents the message of Jesus—the "word" or "good tidings" of the gospel. Christ's message receives a welcome the success of which differs according to the heart that receives it. Perhaps it is on a hard roadside where, with no depth, it is not taken in at all and so is unprotected from the hawklike swoop of the devil. (This "roadside," we should note, is not the public highway but the semipublic pathways that traversed Palestinian fields quite commonly.) The gospel also is refused permanent acceptance where it is not taken to heart, or where worldly ambition gives it no chance to grow strong. The overabundant fruitfulness of a spiritual harvest is well exemplified by the wealth of thirty and sixty and a hundred times the original investment, so unwonted in agricultural life.

As already mentioned, the parable is not intended to reflect any fault on the part of the sower, who is God Himself. God is incapable of the injustice of looking for a harvest which He Himself would have hindered by not sowing properly. Another incorrect interpretation would be the belief that the story suggests that the greater part of the human race—three-fourths?—would be lost to eternal salvation. This lesson is not even hinted at in Christ's explanation. Moreover, the parable never tells us how much seed is wasted in the first three cases. If anything, our supposition would be that most of the seed should have fallen on good ground!

Some question might arise in the minds of Christian married folk whether the meanings offered by certain early Church writers reflect less generously on the state of matrimony. These interpretations suggest in general that the life of virginity is the hundredfold, the life of consecrated widowhood the sixtyfold, and the married state, the thirtyfold. We must keep in mind that interpretations of this sort are examples of what is called the applied sense of the Bible. They are subjectively derived from the gospel, not however stated in the gospel as such.

At heart this particular reflection says nothing more than the age-old Christian doctrine on the relative perfection of certain states of life. The virginal state, vowed to God, is in itself more perfect. This does not make the married state *im*perfect. The holiness of the Christian husband and wife is to be found in living out the duties of *their* state of life to perfection, not in empty and discouraging semiselfish worries about their theoretical lower level. The comparison of perfect states of life exists *only in theory*, indicating an approach to God more or less dependent on creatures. In practice *our perfection corresponds to the degree of the love of God in our hearts*, not to our state of life as such.

There are still other lessons suggested by this parable of the sower in addition to those given by the divine author. It can well represent the quiet growth of the kingdom of God, not in showy pomp and military splendor, but in steady peace, slowly overcoming the obstacles of diabolical enmity, human hardness of heart, and secular distractions. It can also typify the various dispositions which we ourselves (or any other disciples of Christ) can harbor. These dispositions are to be neither partially nor completely sterile. We are to put the word of God into action. It must not be received, only to remain unproductive of faith and good works.

THE WEEDS

Mt. 13:24–30

He related to them another parable, saying, "The Kingdom of Heaven may be compared to a man who sowed good seed in his field; but while his men were asleep, his enemy came and over-sowed darnel weed among the wheat, and went away. But when the stalks had sprung up, and produced grain, then the weeds also became evident. Then the servants of the proprietor came and said to him, 'Didst thou not, sir, sow good seed in thy field? Then whence has it the weeds?' And he said to them, 'An enemy has done this.' And the servants asked him, 'Dost thou wish us to gather them up?' 'No!' he said, 'lest in gathering up the weeds you uproot the wheat along with them. Let both grow together until the harvest; and in the harvesttime I will say to the reapers: First collect the weeds, and bind them into bundles to burn them; but gather the wheat into my barn.' "

Mt. 13:36–43

Then, having dismissed the crowds, He went into the house; and His disciples came to Him, saying, "Explain to us the parable of the weeds in the field." In reply He said to them, "The sower of the good seed is the Son of Man; the field is the world; the good seed are the sons of the Kingdom; the darnel weeds are the sons of the Evil One; the enemy who sowed them is the devil; the harvest is the end of the world, and the reapers are angels. Just as the weeds, then, are collected and burned in the fire, so it shall be at the end of the world. The Son of Man will send out His angels, and they shall gather up out of His Kingdom all scandals, and those who commit wickedness, and shall cast them into the furnace of fire; there shall be the weeping, and the grinding of teeth! Then 'shall the just shine out' like the sun in the Kingdom of their Father. He that has ears to hear, let him hear!"

This is variously called the parable of the cockle, the tares, or the darnel weed. It describes the action of a landlord's malicious enemy who during the night sows darnel seed in a wheat field, so as to ruin the harvest. At the direction of the owner the servants permit the weeds to grow up together with the wheat lest in uprooting the one, the other also would be destroyed. At harvesttime the genuine will be separated from the spurious and burned. Jesus later explains to the apostles the application of the story.

Again like a true parable, this particular narrative does not concern itself with realism in all its details. It concentrates on the heart of its lesson; namely, the presence of bad seed (sinners) in the kingdom, its tolerance by God until the Day of Judgment, and the final retribution and reward. The general picture is true to life. Even though the master himself has sowed the seed, he evidently is rich enough to possess servants. However, the parable passes over in silence the possible negligence of these servants in leaving the field unguarded at night. This might seem an egregious oversight, for the man's enemy is clearly known to be malicious and is no ordinary adversary (he is called "*the* enemy"). None the less, the servants are not blamed. Perhaps the reason is that the chief character is the master. The servants act in the story rather as a sort of literary mirror or incidental foil against which the master's plan will have an occasion to reveal itself.

The parable is only too realistic in its description of the malicious overgrowing. This has been used in the Orient for centuries as a means of getting revenge. The weed in this case has been quite certainly identified as darnel—a somewhat poisonous growth which resembles wheat closely until it is mature. Its roots so intertwine with the wheat that their early uprooting would also destroy the wheat. At harvesttime, however, they can be separated with no further fear of damage.

Jesus Himself interpreted the story for His disciples. "The sower of the good seed is the Son of Man." This is the term which He used most frequently in His preaching to designate Himself. It evidently referred to the Messiah, from its use in the prophecy of Daniel (Dan. 7:13). At the same time it was vague enough to prevent its being misunderstood in the temporal sense, as if Jesus were planning to proclaim Himself as a military liberator, rallying the people to throw off the yoke of Rome. We might think of it as meaning that Jesus is *the* member of the human race par excellence, our most outstanding representative linking His divinity with our humanity.

Christ's explanation was occasion for real surprise. One could expect evil in the world, but here the teacher is saying that evil will also exist in His kingdom of God. Only at the end of time will the "angels"—the messengers of the Son of Man, His servants —"gather up out of His Kingdom all scandals, and those who commit wickedness, and shall cast them into the furnace of fire." Thus, Jesus implicitly claims to be the final judge (and therefore clothed with divine power) on the Last Day.

The "furnace of fire" parallels the fire which burns the darnel weed at the harvest. Now, however, it signifies the place of eternal torments, like the furnace of fire in Daniel 3:6. The metaphor of the furnace changes; in hell there shall occur the "weeping and grinding of teeth" of the impenitent. This phrase was already common in Jewish literature in speculations on the lot of the damned. Jesus adopts it here as something already familiar to His listeners, indicating a chattering of teeth from fear and impotent rage. We ourselves must note that these impenitents have determined their sad outcome for themselves. They are not treated unjustly. Because they are hardened in evil, they do not want forgiveness.

Jesus again uses popular Jewish terms to describe the lot of the just: they shall "shine out like the sun in the Kingdom of their Father" (cf. Wisdom 3:7). The closing comment, "He who has ears to hear, let him hear," is a strong way of calling attention to the importance of the preceding words.

As for the lessons of the parable, it seems quite certain that the coexistence of good and evil, tolerated by God even in the Church until the end of time, is paramount. Implicitly, we are told that God will draw greater good out of this master plan than by means of the instant vindication we in our temporal shortsightedness might desire. The unabated malice of the prince of evil makes us realize the power which God permits him to exercise, always, however, within the limits which the divine wisdom has set.

While accepting these lessons, Christian interpretation has never applied this parable to mean that evil is to go unchecked in this world, even though human vigilance could prevent it. Jesus' many directions to the Church to preserve its discipline (elsewhere in the gospel, as, for example, in Mt. 18:18) are ample reason for this stand.

We have already mentioned that Jesus does not blame the servants for negligence in permitting the enemy to sow his weeds. Hence, this avoidance of negligence cannot be said to be a direct lesson of the parable. However, some writers have often made a proper application; namely, that religious shepherds, teachers, and parents must be vigilant lest error and sin treacherously infiltrate to the midst of those in their charge.

THE MUSTARD SEED

Mt. 13:31–32

Another parable He related to them, saying, "The Kingdom of Heaven is like a grain of mustard, which a man took and sowed in his field. It is the smallest of all seeds; but when it is grown, it is the largest of garden herbs, and becomes a tree, so that the birds of the sky come and dwell among its branches."

Mk. 4:30–32

He said also, "To what shall we liken the Kingdom of God, or by what parable shall we illustrate it? It is like a grain of mustard, which, when it is sown in the ground, though it is smaller than any of the seeds that are in the ground, yet, after being sown, it grows up and becomes the largest of all garden herbs, and puts out great branches, so that the birds of the sky can lodge in its shade."

Lk. 13:18–19

And He said, "What is the Kingdom of God like, and to what shall I compare it? It is like a grain of mustard, which a man took and sowed in his own garden; and it grew, and became a tree; and the birds of the sky lodged among its branches."

There is little difficulty in understanding this parable. The mustard seed was well known in Jesus' time and among Jesus' hearers. The smallness of the seed was practically a Jewish proverb symbolizing insignificance. When Jesus calls it "the smallest of all seeds," this is to be understood in the popular sense in which it was uttered. It is an instance of the figure of speech called hyperbole, an exaggeration which is used by a speaker in order to emphasize the strength of his words. The Bible is not to be read as a textbook of botany or any other science. It speaks according to external appearances or even according to the popular way of viewing things, and not according to their internal nature.

The lesson of the parable follows easily. Just as this tiny seed grows into a large bush strong enough to support birds who rest in its branches, so the kingdom of God grows from insignificant beginnings. Implicitly, the parable admonishes us not to be discouraged by the difficulties which the spread of God's word encounters.

In an applied sense many interpretations can be added which are not in the original meaning of Christ. Thus, the branches of the mustard bush can be understood as the preachers whose labors help to magnify the effects of the gospel after its humble origins. Some Christian writers have drawn lessons from the medicinal properties of the mustard, but these must always be accepted as applications at best, and not as part of the parable itself.

THE LEAVEN

Mt. 13:33

He told them another parable: "The Kingdom of Heaven is like leaven, which a woman took and hid in three measures of flour, until the whole was leavened."

Lk. 13:20–21

And again He said, "To what shall I compare the Kingdom of God? It is like leaven, which a woman took and hid in three measures of flour, until the whole was leavened."

This parable, consisting of only one sentence, compares the growth of the Kingdom of Heaven to the silent spread of leaven throughout the mass of dough. The leaven is practically imperceptible at the moment. It is noticed only after enough time has elapsed to produce its ultimately remarkable effect. In this sense, therefore, the importance and the influence of the silent interior spirit of the kingdom are clearly pictured in the parable.

Probably the greatest interest for us lies in the reference to the domestic custom of raising bread before baking it. In times after our Lord the leaven was ordinarily purchased at the baker's shop. Earlier (as undoubtedly in Jesus' day, to judge from His language), the leaven was prepared at home by the housewife. In all probability she saved a small portion of dough from each day's baking, to be mixed with the new dough of the next day. The Romans prepared leaven from a mixture of grape juice and wheat, allowing it to ferment; or else the dough itself was permitted to sour.

The "three measures of flour" into which the small portion of leaven was mixed would equal about a bushel in modern dry measure. By using so large a quantity, the parable makes it very clear that the small amount of leaven increased itself tremendously, as would the kingdom of Jesus. This final dimension, it seems, should not be interpreted as an indication of the final size of the kingdom. It is pertinent only in its value as a relative figure, not the absolute description of the extent of the kingdom.

THE TREASURE

Mt. 13:44
"The Kingdom of Heaven is like a treasure buried in the field, which a man finds and covers up; and in his delight goes and sells all he possesses, and buys that field."

One sentence again is sufficient to sketch a picture illustrating the value of spiritual riches. A man finds a treasure in a field. This discovery was in all likelihood a chest filled with gold, silver, or bronze. Jesus' hearers were well aware that the troubled times of their country led to a practice of burying precious objects until such time as the owner could possess them in safety. We are not told, for the parable is not interested in the detail, precisely how the find was made—whether by a chance plowman or by some other person digging in the field. At any rate the laborer sells all he has in order to buy the field and with it the treasure (which he had covered up). He does all this in sheer delight and with no thought of the sacrifice needed to gain the one thing on which he has set his heart.

The lesson of the parable is in general quite clear. The kingdom of Heaven and its spiritual values are so precious that anyone who realizes their unbelievable worth will gladly sacrifice every worldly possession, every worldly attachment, in order to obtain the spiritual treasure that surpasses all else.

But if the lesson is clear, the parable none the less has carried with it an apparent implicit moral difficulty. Was Jesus praising the deceitful action of the finder, who purchased the field at a low price which was basically unjust, because he knew what the field actually contained? This objection does not hold true, in the first place, as far as Christ's praise might be concerned. The reason is that the parable concentrates on the one lesson of sacrificing all lesser goods in order to obtain what one has realized is the greatest good. The question of the justice of buying the field is a literary detail outside the purview of the parable.

Secondly, perhaps the finder should not be called unjust after all. If he had been a common thief, he would have removed the treasure stealthily under cover of night. Instead, he was honest enough to give the owner what the owner wished to receive for his parcel of land. By our judgment on his conduct he may have acted unjustly according to present-day standards, but while being less perfect he was not in the wrong according to the ancient outlook on a case of this sort. None the less, the parable certainly does not sanction deceit in business transactions whereby hidden defects or enormous values would deliberately be concealed.

Jesus applied the parable to the transcendent values of the kingdom of Heaven. We can understand, therefore, how later commentators have extended this application to any part of the kingdom, so that one becomes eager to sacrifice each and every worldly value for the supreme spiritual treasures of the doctrine of the church, the appreciation of the Holy Eucharist, or the love of the Sacred Heart of Jesus.

THE PEARL OF GREAT PRICE

Mt. 13:45–46

"Again, the Kingdom of Heaven is like a merchant in search of fine pearls; who, having found a single pearl of great value, went and sold all he possessed and bought it."

In another sentence-parable Jesus masterfully compresses a powerful lesson. Again a treasure is at stake, but this time the treasure is not found by accident. It has been deliberately sought by an expert who travels far and wide "in search of fine pearls." He sells all he has in order to buy the pearl he desires. In the same way the spiritual treasures of the kingdom can be deliberately sought by one who earnestly desires to know God's will and to follow it out perfectly. To do God's will, all else, even his own self-will, is to be given up without a thought of regret.

The merchant of this parable has at times been criticized, as if he were greedy for gain by purchasing the pearl. The story Jesus tells does not, however, suggest in the slightest that the man bought the pearl in fraud or that he intended to sell it at great profit. Instead, as an artist of his trade he wishes to own the pearl for its own sake.

We might well note that in the application of this parable the complete self-renunciation symbolized by the merchant does not mean necessarily a drastic and dreadful life of austerity. Centuries of Christian interpretation based on "Blessed are the poor in spirit" have laid emphasis on the interior spirit of renunciation as the essential of renunciation for Christ. A spirit of detachment is therefore what is needed. If and when the demands of duty or generosity in carrying out God's will call for dying to one's selfishness (for that is the meaning of mortification), the scale of values applied by the pearl merchant will hold true even more strongly.

THE FISH NET

Mt. 13:47–50

"Again, the Kingdom of Heaven is like a drag-net which was let down into the sea, and collected fishes of every kind; then, when it was filled, they drew it up on the beach, and sitting down they picked out the good into vessels, and cast the bad away. So shall it be at the end of the world. The angels shall go forth and separate the wicked from among the just, and shall cast them into the furnace of fire; there shall be the weeping and the grinding of teeth!"

In this parable Jesus draws a comparison between the work of fishermen who sort the bad fish from the good, and the angels at the end of the world who separate the wicked from the just. The lesson of this parable is closely allied to that of the parable of the darnel weed. Much of what we said there applies equally well here, especially with respect to the coexistence of good and evil in the kingdom of God until the day of judgment with its "furnace of fire" and "grinding of teeth" destined for the impenitent. It is notable that Jesus for all His lovable meekness feels impelled to repeat here the description of hell.

Jesus calls His kingdom itself the drag-net which collects fishes of every kind. His parable is very true to life when it reminds His listeners of a scene they had witnessed so often at the shores of Lake Gennesaret. The "bad" fish would be those too small to keep, and those legally unclean according to Jewish dietary law, that is, not having scales.

No interpretation is valid which would seek to wrest from this parable the revelation of God's eternal secret concerning the number of the saved. Our reason for this statement is primarily the fact of Christ's refusals to give the apostles a direct answer to their questions on that score. Theoretically, the parable could be explained as if most of the fish were retained, and therefore good, for fishermen could not make a living from catches which had a high percentage of discards. On the other hand, the equally justified impression implicit in the parable is that a sizable amount were actually lost. Our conclusion must be based on the purpose of the parable, and that is the lesson of the darnel weed. God tolerates evil to exist together with good in the kingdom of Christ on earth until the Last Day. We note that here Jesus does not mention (as He did in the parable of the weeds) the authoritative part of the Son of Man in the final judgment. Instead, the work is delegated to angels.

THE SEED GROWING QUIETLY

Mk. 4:26–29

He said, moreover, "The Kingdom of God is as if a man should cast seed into the ground, and should sleep and rise night and day, and the seed should sprout and grow, he knows not how. The earth yields crops of its own accord; first the blade, then the ear, then the full grain in the ear. But when the crop is ripe, he immediately puts in the sickle, because the harvest is come."

This, the last of the parables of the seed and the kingdom, is found only in the gospel of Mark. We notice at the outset that Mark, writing for a gentile audience probably at Rome, speaks of the Church of Christ as the "Kingdom of God" instead of the "Kingdom of Heaven." As mentioned earlier, Mark has put Jesus' words into the non-Semitic expression so that they would be better understood.

The kingdom, the parable says, is like seed cast into the ground.

A notable phrase then occurs. While the sower would "sleep and rise night and day," the seed would sprout and grow, "*he knows not how.*" After the earth has matured its crops of its own accord, the sower puts in his sickle because the time for harvest has arrived.

We might think at first sight that this parable merely repeats the lesson, for example, of the leaven, which permeates the mass of dough silently yet effectively. However, the new element introduced here in the interior process of growth. Applied to Christ, who is evidently the sower, the parable means that He begins His Church, and then lets it continue more or less by human means, with His visible presence no longer helping it. In any event His terrestrial kingdom as Messiah will not be perfectly realized at once, despite the fond hopes of the disciples who mistakenly looked forward to the utter rout of the foreign Roman rulers. Only at the end of time will Jesus return to reap the harvest of the kingdom in which He has so much interest. Implicitly, therefore, Jesus as the founder of the kingdom is claiming the divine authority of conducting the harvest, the Last Judgment.

It would be absurd were we to apply *all* the details of the narrative to the divine sower. As God, He certainly does not sleep and rise from His work. Most of all, His spiritual harvest does not develop in a way unknown to Him and outside His control.

The present parable does not mean that once we have begun a project, we should let matters take their course without our constant watchfulness. Such an attitude would be one of undue presumption, a failure to take the necessary natural means which God in His providence wishes us to use.

In a spiritual sense the parable can be a source of encouragement not only for the spiritual shepherds of Christ's Church but also for all who work in any way to spread Christ's kingdom. Our labors of helping to sow Christ's word have a certain automatic effect or culmination. Despite the fact that we perceive no visible effects in every case, the spiritual harvest quietly ripens inde-

pendently of our efforts. We might remind ourselves in this connection, therefore, that our sowing of the seed is all that we do.
Someone else will water it, and God alone will give the increase.

It is interesting to note the botanical observations Jesus has
added for His listeners, folk who knew the growing of grain so
well: "first the blade, then the ear, then the full grain in the ear."
Need we remark still again that the parable does not apply these
picturesque steps of growth to the kingdom? It would be only in
an extended sense, as a subjective interpretation, if we were to
claim that a particular century in the history of the church represents the blade; another century, the ear; and still another, the
end to come. Such a claim would be contrary to Christ's teaching
in so far as He steadfastly refused to give any hint when the end
of the world will come. Apart from statements veiled in the obscurity of prophetic figures, His reply to all such queries was the
admonition to watch and be ready for His coming.

THE PRUDENT HOUSEHOLDER

Mt. 13:52
"Every teacher trained in the Kingdom of Heaven is like the
master of a family, who brings out from his storehouse new things
and old."

This single sentence of Jesus for all its shortness has been the
occasion for inversely proportionate obscurity. The word translated here from the Greek as "teacher" appears in older English
translations as "scribe." It is understandable how a modern reader
of such a translation finds it hard to think of the disciples as
"scribes"—a name so often linked in the gospels with the Pharisees.

One's mind has to leap too far. Hence, the expression is much more aptly turned as "teacher" instead of "scribe"—one, namely, who is well instructed in the doctrines of Christ's kingdom.

The entire reference to the "master of a family" or prudent householder should technically be listed as a compressed parable rather than as a fully developed narrative lesson. Jesus had just finished His series of parables of the kingdom (and that is why we discuss this parable here, at the end of our opening series). Apparently He was satisfied that His disciples were beginning to grasp the outlines of His portrayal of the spiritual kingdom which differed so drastically from their earlier temporal ideas. *Therefore,* He added, *because* the disciples understood it, they now possessed new knowledge of the new law of love in addition to the old law which had been their heritage.

The "storehouse" of the householder has appeared in some English translations as "treasury," again with a burden of being obscure. The correct idea is that the master of the house protects his many possessions in an inner room where the recently acquired is kept together with what was got long before. In the application of the parable the storeroom would be the hearts of the disciples where all the good of the Old Testament is brought to its perfection by being mixed with the good of the New. One is reminded here of Jesus' words in the Sermon on the Mount which express the same idea, "Do not imagine that I have come to abolish the Law or the Prophets; I have come not to abolish, but to fulfil" (Mt. 5:17).

HOUSES WITH FIRM FOUNDATIONS

Mt. 7:24–27

"Every one, therefore, who listens to these words of Mine, and puts them in practice, shall be compared to a wise man who built his house upon the rock; and the rain descended, and the floods came, and the winds blew, and beat upon that house, and it fell not, for it had been founded upon the rock. And every one who listens to these words of Mine, but does not put them into practice, shall be compared to a foolish man, who built his house upon the sand; and the rain descended, and the floods came, and the winds blew, and dashed against that house, and it fell; and utter was its ruin!"

Lk. 6:47–49

"Every one who comes to Me, and listens to My words, and puts them into practice—I will show you whom he is like. He is like a man building a house, who dug, and kept deepening, and laid a foundation upon rock. And when a flood came, the torrent broke upon that house, and could not shake it; for it had been well built. But he who listens and does not practice, is like a man building a house upon the ground without a foundation; against which the torrent broke, and at once it fell; and the wreck of that house was utter."

Both Matthew and Luke relate this parable, but Luke does not include in his passage the reference which Jesus made to a house built on sand. Instead, Luke summarizes the idea by speaking of such a house as "without a foundation." The parable occurs at the end of the Sermon on the Mount.

After having expounded so much doctrine, Jesus wished to emphasize that His teaching was to lead to action and was not to stop short with a merely verbal asquiescence. What he said, moreover, was of such permanent value and truth that it would uphold anyone who accepted it amid all the troubles of life. In other words it was like the rock foundation of a house. If, however, people disregarded Christ's words and decided to lead their lives according to worldly principles that sought the passing good of the present moment and neglected the eternal truths, their lives would be as unstable as the house built on sand.

This parable is one of the easiest to understand because the terms of its comparison are so vivid and so easily applied. Of interest to us moderns would be the customs of house construction then in vogue. Each man was his own architect and builder. A house on a hillside would logically be of rock and excavated back into the hill to provide a rear cave-like room. In flat areas, however, the builder would have to dig through the sand or loose earth on the surface in order to reach stronger ground. His time-saving and labor-saving haste of neglecting a deep foundation would be his ruin in the end. The cloudbursts of the October-November rainy season would cause torrential floods that would wash away all but the solid constructions.

As usual, Jesus is the skillful artist in words as He mentions to His listeners the series of trying conditions: "The rains fell, the floods came, and the winds blew, and dashed against that house, and it fell!" These literary touches are evidently not part of the lesson of the parable. Its general lesson is, as we have said, the need for sound doctrine. The parable is not so allegorical as to draw further lessons regarding the significance of the rains, the floods, and the winds in the supernatural life.

THE TWO DEBTORS

Lk. 7:41–43

"A certain money-lender had two debtors, one of whom owed him five hundred denarii, and the other fifty. As they had nothing with which to pay, he freely forgave them both. Which of them, now, would love him more?"

The confusion that has resulted from surface reading of this parable demands a careful study of Jesus' thought. For a popular exposition such as this intends to be, it seems also imperative to discuss the further logical question as to the identity of the penitent woman mentioned in the narrative.* We shall consider the parable first.

In all likelihood the episode of the anonymous penitent woman occurred some time during the second year of Jesus' public life. The place was the city of Capharnaum in Galilee, the northern third of Palestine. Jesus had been invited to dine at the home of a man named Simon, who was a member of the Pharisee sect. At banquets of this sort the Jews had adopted the custom of reclining on pillows or low couches set diagonally away from the table. While resting on the left elbow, they would eat with the right hand. This arrangement helps us understand how the diners' feet could conveniently be washed (as Christ Himself washed the feet of the apostles at the Last Supper), since the feet were away from the table, contrary to our modern custom of sitting during meals.

While the banquet was in progress, a woman known to be a prostitute entered the room, bathed Jesus' feet with her tears, wiped them with her hair, kissed His feet, and then anointed them with perfumed oil. Simon the host inwardly grumbled to himself.

* For the question of the identity of the anonymous penitent woman, of Mary Magdalen, and of Mary of Bethany, cf. Lk. 7:36–50; Lk. 8:2–3; Mt. 26:6–13; Mk. 14:3–9; Jn. 12:1–8; Jn. 11:1–2. See the discussion, pages 37–41.

Such conduct, he thought, indicated a lack of prophetical insight on Christ's part, as to the nature of the woman who was touching Him. Jesus read his thoughts and then told him the parable of the two debtors.

Each of two debtors owed a moneylender 500 and 50 "denarii" respectively. (The denarius was formerly calculated at about $0.17 in American money. Fluctuations in purchasing power make this figure no longer accurate, but we could use $85 and $8.50 as reasonable sums to indicate the relative size of the two debts.) The moneylender, evidently out of generosity, forgave both men the amount which each of them had been unable to repay. Jesus did not conclude the parable Himself, but adroitly asked Simon which of the two loved his benefactor more. Simon rightly supposed that the one to whom more was forgiven would have more gratitude, and therefore more love, than the one who received a lesser favor.

At this point in the parable we must stop to appraise the logic for what it is worth. If we were to apply the lesson to the forgiveness of sin, we could not justly say that greater sinners automatically love God more because more sins have been forgiven them than the saints whose lives have been characterized by spotless innocence. The reason is that the love of the saints has been the motivating force keeping them from sin. But the parable is not intent on that particular application. Jesus merely wishes to make the point that gratitude will normally increase according to the benefits granted.

To return to Luke's narrative, we find the paradox of the story beginning to form. Jesus calls Simon's attention to the fact that although He had been an invited guest, no slave washed His feet, and He received none of the customary courtesies: the special kiss of welcome, and anointment. Simon had in cavalier fashion invited Jesus as if to embarrass Him by offering only the barest essentials given to a guest. But this woman, Jesus adds, has proffered the loving services which the host had denied Him; nay, she has offered much more because of her sincerity and generosity.

The next words of Christ seem to invert the lesson of the parable of the two debtors. "Her sins, which are many, are forgiven, because she has loved much; but he to whom little is forgiven loves but little." It is paramount to notice here the casual way in which Jesus speaks of the forgiveness of sins. He makes no apology for the fact that He evidently has the divine authority to do so. But should her sins have been forgiven her *because* she loved much? Did not the parable imply that *because* her sins were forgiven, her love should follow?

The answer here is not a question of strict logic, for Jesus actually compresses several conclusions and emerges with a final conclusion in the practical order that summarizes all that went before. He is saying, then, that the woman's love led her to perform the many penitential actions which won for her the forgiveness she desired. Her sins were forgiven *afterward*, because she had loved Jesus much and in that spirit asked for pardon *beforehand*. At the same time Jesus delicately thrusts another conclusion for Simon himself to make. Simon had thought earlier that this woman was a sinner, far worse than he; Jesus implicitly grants the truth of the assumption. But the Lord promptly takes this fact of lesser guilt (in Simon) to use it as a proof of lesser love!

Jesus ends the scene by explicitly telling the woman her sins are forgiven. The diners are not blind to the meaning of such a claim, and practically challenge its validity. Jesus answers them not with any sort of retraction but with the reiterated assurance of pardon, "Thy faith has saved thee; go in peace." Throughout the entire narrative we can sense the prudence Jesus used in making His claim of divinity. Since His time for persecution unto death had not yet come, He would not teach the fact of His godhead in such an open way as to provide His enemies with material for a charge of blasphemy. Instead, His actions and words formed quasi-premises, the conclusion of which had to be drawn by His listeners. It was a clear, safe course, calculated to permit His apostolate to continue.

THE IDENTITY OF THE ANONYMOUS PENITENT WOMAN

Lk. 7:36–50

One of the Pharisees having asked Him to dine with him, He entered the Pharisee's house, and reclined at table. And behold, a woman who was a sinner in the city, on learning that He was at table in the Pharisee's house, brought an alabaster flask of perfumed oil, and standing behind at His feet weeping, began to bathe His feet with her tears and wipe them with the hair of her head, while she kissed His feet, and anointed them with the perfume.

But the Pharisee who had invited Him, on seeing this, said to himself, "If this Man were a prophet, He would have recognized who and what kind of woman it is who is touching Him; that, in fact, she is a sinner." . . . He then said to her, "Thy sins are forgiven." Those who dined with Him, however, began to say to themselves, "Who is this, who even forgives sins?" But He said to the woman, "Thy faith has saved thee; go in peace."

Lk. 8:2–3

And the Twelve accompanied Him, as well as some women who had been cured of evil spirits and sicknesses—Mary, called the Magdalene, from whom seven demons had gone out, Joanna, wife of Chusa, Herod's steward, Susanna, and many others, who assisted Him out of their own means.

Mt. 26:6–13

Now, when Jesus was at Bethany in the house of Simon the Leper, a woman came to Him with an alabaster flask of a very costly perfumed oil, which she poured upon His head as He reclined at table. . . . Jesus, perceiving it, however, said to them, "Why do you trouble the woman, since she has done Me a noble need? . . . For she, in pouring this perfume upon My body, has done it for My burial. . . ."

Mk. 14:3–9

Now, when He was at Bethany in the house of Simon the Leper, as He was reclining at table, a woman came with an alabaster flask of very costly oil of pure nard; and breaking the flask, she poured it upon His head. . . .

Jn. 12:1–8

Jesus, therefore, six days before the Passover, went to Bethany, where Lazarus was, whom Jesus had raised from the dead. So they gave a supper there in His honor, and Martha attended to the serving, while Lazarus was one of those who reclined at table with Him. Mary, then, taking a pound of very costly oil of pure nard, anointed the feet of Jesus, and wiped His feet with her hair; and the house was filled with the perfume of the oil. . . .

Jn. 11:1–2

Now a certain Lazarus of Bethany, from the village of Mary and her sister Martha, was sick; and it was the Mary who anointed the Lord with perfumed oil, and wiped His feet with her hair, whose brother Lazarus was sick.

Closely allied to the parable of the debtors is the question of the woman's identity. She is popularly taken to be Mary Magdalen and perhaps the same, too, as Mary of Bethany. However, we are presenting the opinion here that these are really *three* different persons, representing

1. *this anonymous penitent woman;*
2. *Mary from Bethany*, who was the sister of Martha and Lazarus;
3. *Mary from Magdala* (a town in Galilee), who was with Jesus on Calvary and after His resurrection.

The opinion we are describing has been held by writers of the Church in the East, while the opposite view identifying all three women as one has been more prevalent in the West since the time of Gregory the Great in the sixth century. Our English language, too, has adopted the identification. A "magdalen" is defined in the dictionary as a "reformed prostitute."

Whether the question can ever be definitely settled is a moot point. The common opinion of biblical scholars today is that no evidence exists in the gospels to support the contention that one woman appears several times with different names.

Why were these three thought to be the same person? The seventh chapter of Luke tells of "a woman who was a sinner in the city," who "began to bathe His feet with her tears and wipe them with the hair of her head, while she kissed His feet and anointed them with the perfume." Luke's eighth chapter begins with the mention of "Mary, called the Magdalene, from whom seven demons had gone out." Would not this indicate that she was the great sinner? John's eleventh chapter tells of Lazarus of Bethany, "from the village of Mary and her sister Martha . . . and it was the Mary who anointed the Lord with perfumed oil, and wiped His feet with her hair. . . ." The case seems to be even stronger when the gospel of Matthew (26:6–13) and the gospel of Mark (14:3–9) tell of this anointing of Jesus, without naming Mary of Bethany and therefore possibly suggesting by this anonymity the anonymous penitent sinner of Luke (7:37).

Many replies, however, can be given to these claims. First of all, "seven demons" or "seven devils" is a biblical way of saying

39

that Mary Magdalen had been possessed by evil spirits in a very tenacious way, from which Jesus freed her. The wording by no means indicates that such a person is a great sinner. Other women are described in the gospels as having had devils possessing them, but these women are never considered as sinners (Lk. 8:2).

Luke speaks of the anonymous penitent sinner in his seventh chapter. His eighth chapter (chapter and verse divisions date only from the thirteenth and sixteenth centuries) opens a completely new block of material, and Mary Magdalen is spoken of as if for the first time, as one being introduced to the narrative. How would Magdalen be the sinner if, after having been described at great length, in a few sentences later she is a new, strange character in the story? Suppose it is claimed (as it has been) that Luke suppressed Magdalen's name in Chapter 7 out of regard for her reputation? Why then would he have mentioned her immediately thereafter as "Mary Magdalene" if his reference to her "seven demons" would have betrayed the secret?

It is even harder to identify the anonymous penitent with Mary of Bethany. Bethany is in the south of Palestine, a good one hundred miles south of the city of Capharnaum, where the sinner broke in on Jesus' banquet. As for "Mary from Magdala," current opinion thinks that Magdala was a town on Lake Gennesaret, also in the north and equally far from Bethany. Mary of Bethany, therefore, would seem to be neither the anonymous penitent nor Mary Magdalen.

We fully agree that confusion could occur at first sight, because Mary of Bethany *also* anointed Jesus at a banquet, and this banquet *also* was in the house of a man named Simon. But Simon is a relatively common name in the Bible, and this man was called Simon the Leper, not Simon who was a Pharisee. The time when his banquet occurred was some six days before Jesus died. Yet the banquet given in the *north* in Galilee by Simon the *Pharisee* (which the sinful woman interrupted) had happened at least a year earlier.

Mary of Bethany came from a good family of evident high reputation. She and her sister Martha and their brother Lazarus had been close friends of Jesus. At "her" banquet given by Simon the Leper, she shed no tears over Jesus. She stayed until the end of the meal. But the anonymous penitent woman was known as a public sinner in the city. At "her" banquet she wept for her sins, and did not stay as part of the banquet party. Thus, John's eleventh chapter describing the anointing of Jesus by a "Mary" refers to a *different* event at a *different* time involving a *different* person from the anonymous sinner.

The confusion in identifying these three women is actually an instance of using the mathematical statement, "Two things equal to a third thing are equal to each other." In this case *Mary* of Bethany is supposed to be another name for *Mary* Magdalen. The banquet at the house of *Simon* the Pharisee is supposed to be the same as the one with *Simon* the Leper. Because one woman—the sinner—wept when she *anointed* Jesus with perfume as a sign of her repentance, this is thought to be the same action as when another woman—Mary of Bethany—*anointed* Jesus (with no weeping) as a sign of honor to Him. The *anonymous woman* in Matthew (26) and Mark (14) is thought to be the same as the *anonymous woman* in Luke (7), both of whom anointed Jesus but under the different circumstances just mentioned. Finally, the devil's influence on one person—Mary Magdalen—is thought to mean that she was the devil's slave in sin.

Hence, we conclude that the repentant sinner whose dramatic interruption of Simon's banquet was the occasion for the parable of the two debtors should not be identified as Mary Magdalen, but should remain in the namelessness Luke mercifully decided to bestow upon her.

THE GOOD SAMARITAN

Lk. 10:30–37

"A man, on his way down from Jerusalem to Jericho, fell among robbers, who both stripped and beat him, and then departed leaving him half dead. Now by chance a certain priest was going down that road, who, at sight of him, passed by on the other side. Likewise, a Levite also, when he came to the place and saw him, passed by on the other side. But a certain Samaritan who was traveling came to where he was, and on seeing him took pity on him, and went to him and bandaged his wounds, pouring on oil and wine. Then seating him on his own beast he conveyed him to an inn, and took care of him. And the next day, taking out two denarii, he gave them to the landlord, and said, 'Take care of him; and whatever thou dost spend besides, I will pay thee on my return.' Which of these three, dost thou think, proved neighbor to him who fell among the robbers?" He who performed the work of mercy on him," was the reply. "Go," said Jesus to him, "and do the like thyself."

It will be noticed that whereas Matthew records parables that deal with the founding and growth of the kingdom of Christ, Luke almost exclusively has preserved for us the lengthy parables with moral lessons, such as we are examining in the present section.

The parable of the Good Samaritan has been acclaimed with so many superlatives in all Christian centuries that one wonders whether or how any comment can be made worthy of the original narrative. The lesson is direct and easy to draw. Most of our interest will lie in understanding the background of the story as well as the psychology of the divine teacher who proposed it.

The section begins with a question from a scribe, a teacher of the law, "Master, what must I do in order to inherit eternal life?"

The gospel expression stating that this was done "to test Him," does not necessarily mean that the question was a trap. The idea rather was to test Jesus' answer by experiment. Therefore, the question seems to have been placed in good will.

Jesus is always the master in any dialogue or repartee. A student of the art of debating could find all the skills of orderly and persuasive argument in Christ's words. In this instance He answers the question by another question, whereby the lawyer is made to answer his own query: "What is written in the law?" The only reply the lawyer can make is to quote from the Book of Deuteronomy (6:5), on the precept of loving God with all one's being. Every Jew would know this, for it was part of the Shema, the prayer to be recited twice daily. But the lawyer added the next phrase, "Thou shalt love thy neighbor as thyself" (from Lev. 19:18), on his own. Here is additional evidence of his good will, for the love of a non-Jew drew little attention from official commentators.

We are somewhat puzzled, therefore, to read the next question, "And who is my neighbor?" put forward in an effort "to justify himself." As a solution to this difficulty it has been suggested that the lawyer himself desired a more liberal doctrine teaching greater love of *all* men than was taught in his surroundings. Now, then, he would propose his question to the young, brilliant rabbi Jesus, and thus hope to receive some confirmation of his belief.

Strikingly, our Lord does not answer the question point-blank, but begins instead the story of the man on his way from Jerusalem to Jericho who fell among robbers, was stripped, beaten, and left half dead. Since this is taught in parabolic style, it seems more probable that Jesus is not describing an actual robbery as such. It was, however, something so very likely that His listeners would accept it as a very probable case in real life. The road from Jerusalem to Jericho descends from a height of some three thousand feet, and in the time of Jesus was about twenty miles long. It traversed territory so wild that the desolate hills afforded brigands excellent lairs for swift ambush and equally swift retreat to the wilderness. The road, moreover, was the only possible route and thus was sure to carry rich traffic.

The victim in the parable is evidently a Jew. For that reason there was little or no possible justification of national prejudice for the priest and the Levite to pass him by without a gesture of pity or help. The priest by his calling should have been particularly sensitive to the needs of others. The Levite as an inferior minister of the temple at Jerusalem shared the same responsibility. Their "chance" meeting with the unfortunate meant nothing to them as an occasion for mercy.

The Samaritan enters the parable at this point. We must remember that violent hostility existed between the Jews and the Samaritans. It dated back partly to the period after the Assyrian invasion of Palestine some seven centuries earlier, when the conquerors of Samaria had introduced aliens who intermarried with the remnants of the Jews left behind. A greater cause of friction occurred over the rival temple which the Samaritans later constructed on Mount Gerazim. The mutual hatred was so intense that each faction avoided the other's territory as much as possible, and would normally prefer traveling around rather than through the other's country.

The Samaritan forgets all nationalist hatred as he takes pity on the beaten man, bandaging his wounds and pouring on oil and wine. Jesus is meticulous in mentioning each act of service: meeting, taking pity, bandaging, pouring medicament, seating on his beast, conveying to an inn, taking care of him. There can be little doubt that the dear Lord had a definite lesson in mind!

The bandages would come from strips of the Samaritan's own clothing; the oil and wine from his provisions could be used also as healing and antiseptic agents, to use a modern term. The beast in the parable is probably an ass. Since the Samaritan owns it himself, he would be a relatively prosperous businessman.

We must rid ourselves of occidental notions when we think of the inn of Christ's time. The Greek word used in the gospels describes it as "a place of welcome for all"—and that was practically all that such inns could be called. Actually a shelter for the night, the typical inn consisted of a stockade protected by a stout gate. Porticos along the wall covered the guests, who would sleep on the ground fully dressed, while their mounts were tethered nearby.

In giving two denarii to the innkeeper, the Samaritan left with him the equivalent of two days' pay, promising to fill out any extra debt upon his return trip. We do not intend to be irreverent in citing the following "modern" comment on this part of the parable, which has its value in illustrating the skeleton outline of the typical parable.

At any rate, a twentieth century jocose interpretation reminds us how far removed the parable is from the soap-opera effect of daily serials on radio and television, each ending on a note of suspense. Did the Samaritan recoup the losses of the robbed man by apprehending the thieves? Did the robbed man recover? Did the Samaritan return to pay the innkeeper? Was the innkeeper honest in caring for his wounded and helpless charge? For the parable, queries such as these are otiose; the parable simply forgets details when they do not pertain to the main lesson for whose sake it has been composed.

Jesus is now ready to give His answer to the lawyer. Yet, even now, the answer is again in the form of a question. "Which of these, dost thou think, proved neighbor to him who fell among robbers?" Again, it lifts apparent good will to greater heights. "He who performed the work of mercy on him," comes the reply. The lawyer had been sincere at least in citing the obligation of loving one's neighbor, but he seemed to be thinking of what *rights* were owed him rather than the *duties* he owed to others. Jesus makes the closing comment, "Go, and do the like thyself."

There can be no doubt that this definition of one's neighbor—namely, *everyone*, particularly when in need—is the chief lesson of the parable. In an applied and allegorical sense great Fathers of the Church have taken each detail and have drawn new lessons. The man wounded by the robbers is mankind wounded by sin; the Good Samaritan is Jesus; the inn is the Church; and the Good Samaritan will return at the Last Judgment. One cannot deny the beauty of these applications, though always remembering, of course, that they are not taught as such in the parable.

THE IMPORTUNATE FRIEND

Lk. 11:5–8
He then said to them, "Suppose one of you has a friend, to whom he goes at midnight and says, 'Friend, lend me three loaves; for a friend of mine has arrived at my house from a journey, and I have nothing to set before him'; and he, answering from within, says, 'Don't bother me; the door is now fastened, and my children and I are in bed; I cannot get up and give them to you.' I tell you, though he will not get up and give them to him because he is his friend, yet because his friend persists, he will rise and give him as many as he needs."

Among the parables teaching moral lessons, this story of the persistent friend was used by Jesus as an example of perseverance in prayer. It is not phrased in the explicit form Jesus sometimes used, as if He had said, "Perseverance in prayer is like the conduct of the man who woke his friend at midnight. . . ." Instead, its fanciful nature is indicated by the beginning words, "Suppose one of you has a friend."

The background of the parable is the proper hospitality to be shown to a traveler. Since he arrives at midnight, the traveler must have chosen nighttime for his journey, evidently to avoid the heat of the summer day. His host, however, has no food on hand; the day's baking of bread has been eaten. The host accordingly goes to a friend's house in the neighborhood and wakens the owner. The reception he gets is hardly a friendly welcome, even though the reason for his disturbance is sensible enough. Loud knocking on the door finally has produced its effect; grumbling can be heard from within.

The householder alleges that he cannot be of service—and the people listening to the parable would have little trouble visualizing the situation inside. Typically, such a house's door was massively locked with cumbersome bolts and bars. The children of the family were asleep on mats placed on the hard-packed mud floor, dressed in their ordinary gown-like clothes of the day. (Only the rich could afford special clothes for the night.) To open the door would mean waking several sleepy, touseled heads.

None the less, it is quite evident by this time that the irritable householder is more reluctant than hampered. His "I cannot" is really "I will not." The bond of friendship is not strong enough to make him forget his inconvenience. But the constant knocking of the man making the request is such a nuisance that finally he rises and gives his nocturnal visitor not just the three loaves which he asks, but "as many as he needs." The loaves mentioned would be about eight inches in diameter, and a half-inch thick. Three loaves would have been enough for a meal.

The moral is certainly perseverance in prayer. Jesus insinuates this lesson in advance when He says that persistence accomplished in the parable what friendship alone was unable to do. But the Lord made His own point very explicit when He added, "Ask, and it shall be given you; seek, and you shall find; knock, and it shall be opened to you. For every one who asks receives, and he who seeks finds, and to him who knocks it shall be opened." (Lk. 11:9–10; Mt. 7:7–8).

The proper attitude toward petition to God is so closely connected with the next parable Luke tells that we shall also discuss it next, instead of repeating ideas first suggested here and developed more fully there. The present parable, however, must not be interpreted in any sense that would reflect a lack of perfection and love on God's part. God, symbolized by the awakened householder, is certainly not indifferent to the needs of His creatures or irritated at being asked for help. Moreover, God as our friend is always more generous than we are, and we can never do more in serving Him than He has done and will do for us. Hence, the details of the parable cannot apply to Him, as if He would not hear our prayers out of love for us, but would do so only after a series of half-superstitious babblings had pestered Him to grant our requests if only they were mechanically continued long enough.

THE SON ASKING FOR BREAD

Mt. 7:9–11

"What man is there among you, who, if his son asks him for a loaf of bread, will hand him a stone? Or, if he asks for a fish, will hand him a serpent? If you, then, who are sinful, know how to bestow good gifts upon your children, how much more will your Father who is in heaven bestow benefits on those who ask Him!"

Lk. 11:11–13

"Suppose one of you asks his father for a loaf of bread—will he hand him a stone? Or for a fish—will he instead of a fish hand him a serpent? Or if he asks for an egg—will he hand him a scorpion? If then you, who are sinful, know how to bestow kind gifts on your children, how much more will your heavenly Father impart the Holy Spirit to those who ask Him?"

This compressed parable is placed by Luke shortly after the Lord's Prayer. Matthew groups it with Jesus' exhortation to prayer in the Sermon on the Mount. Like its immediate predecessor and twin parable in Luke, the present story is a simple supposition, not a flat statement that one thing is like something else. In this case, Jesus juxtaposes a son's request for a loaf of bread or a fish or an egg, and asks the rhetorical question how any true father could give to his son a stone instead, or a serpent or a scorpion.

In explaining this parable efforts have been made at times to correlate bread and stone, fish and serpent, and egg and scorpion, as if the one looked so much like the other that a mistake could easily be made in distinguishing them. It seems better to decide that Jesus merely wished to indicate articles diametrically opposed to the beneficial foods which the son asked for. Then came the strongly worded conclusion. If human fathers, "who are sinful," know how to bestow gifts on their children, how much more will not the Eternal Father in Heaven impart the "Holy Spirit" (as Luke reports the phrase) and "benefits" (according to Matthew) to those who ask Him!

Whereas the preceding parable of the importunate friend emphasized the need for perseverance in prayer, this parable brings forward the absolute goodness and fidelity of God in answering prayer. The comparison is so powerfully worded that theoretically one can feel not the slightest hesitation in believing that God will give us what is good for us. But Jesus realized the difficulty of faith, how hard it would be in the practical order for us to live out this lesson of complete trust in God's bounty. Hence, He used so bald a comparison. How, indeed, could a human father do more for his son than God does for us!

Notably, Luke says that the benefits of God would be the "good" or "holy" spirit of God in answer to our prayer. This evidently is Luke's way of pointing out that no possible benefit is greater than this. Matthew's reference to "benefits" implicitly reminds us that the prayer of petition is not to be condemned as something imperfect or selfish, provided our prayers are not made up solely of "give me this, give me that."

Jesus' phrase "you who are sinful" does not seem to be intended as a reprimand to the listeners. From the context, it appears more likely as a statement of fact which they themselves should have been the first ones to admit. Mankind for all its sinfulness and selfishness none the less can and does perform very good deeds; by a parallel, how much good must not God do, for He is without sin or stain!

One wonders how Jesus could have spoken more forcibly of the fact that our prayers are heard by God. To speak colloquially, the Lord burned His bridges behind Him. He left no outlet, no subterfuge, no plausible interpretation whereby any one of us could claim that God fails to hear sincere and persevering prayer. On this score, we should recall all Christian tradition concerning the prayer of petition. Jesus divinely and infallibly made His promises; what can we say if our prayers do not seem to be heard?

The answers have been given by commentators down through the centuries. Perhaps we have asked for something not good for us, or we have not asked in the proper way. "Proper way" here means the sincerity which would make our prayer a candid, loving request. It means the generosity which would make us steadfast in asking. It means, finally, the requesting of our needs in a spirit of respect owed to an all-loving father. If, then, according to our conscience we have offered our prayers in the proper way, then the only conclusion we can draw (if our prayers have not been granted) is that either we have asked for something which would harm us, or else it would harm us if given at this precise time.

It is striking to note that in all Christ's promises that prayer would be heard, Jesus never once indicated *when* the petitions would be granted. On the *fact* of our being heard, Jesus was, as we have insisted, mightily eloquent, never leaving the slightest doubt about His meaning. It is only on this point of the *time* when our prayers are to be granted that He was silent.

Someone has said that according to our Lord's promises, God *hears* all our prayers, God *answers* all our prayers, but God does not necessarily *grant* all our prayers if their petition is not for our good. Perhaps an ideal way to conclude these reflections on the parables of prayer is to quote a statement always apropos in a context like this. It is ascribed to a Confederate soldier:

"I asked God for help that I might do greater things; I was given infirmity that I might do better things. I asked for all things that I might enjoy life; I was given life that I might enjoy all things. I received nothing that I asked for, but everything I had hoped for. Despite myself, my prayers are answered. I am, among all men, most richly blessed."

THE RICH FOOL

Lk. 12:16–21

"The land of a certain rich man produced abundant crops; and he reflected within himself, 'What shall I do? for I have nowhere to store my crops. This is what I will do,' said he; 'I will pull down my storehouses and build larger ones; and there I will store up all my produce and my goods. Then I will say to my soul, O soul, thou hast plenty of wealth laid up for many years; take thine ease, eat, drink, be merry!' But God said to him, 'Thou fool! this night thy soul is required of thee; then whose shall be the things with which thou hast provided thyself?' So it is with one who hoards wealth for himself, and is not rich toward God."

Luke's introduction, "He then told them a parable," reminds us once again that the Hebrew parable was often much more a story with a general lesson than a strictly compared twin account. Jesus' picture is simple. A rich landowner thinks only of amassing worldly wealth so that he can have an abundance of earthly pleasures in the many years ahead of him, but he dies on the very night of his decision. His foolishness consisted in amassing a fortune that actually went to someone else after him. He was negligent in building up spiritual wealth for himself, wealth which would last forever.

The "crops" in the parable are not identified; probably they were wheat. The "storehouses" which the owner wrecked in order to build even larger ones would be simple covered areas, with sides of stilts or stones. The man's reference to his "soul" merely meant himself, for the Semitic mind of our Lord's time did not make the distinctions of Greek philosophy on the differences between spirit and matter.

We should notice that the rich man did not obtain his wealth by sinful means. Even his plan for the future cannot be called explicitly sinful in itself: "eat, drink, be merry," although the luxury of such worldliness would probably have led him into evil. The sinfulness he manifests lies in his absolute neglect of the law of God, with all the emphasis on himself even to the added neglect of the needs of the poor.

The parable dramatically gives us a vivid tableau, *as if* God were to address him directly, "Thou fool!" We say "as if," because here again we are dealing with a parabolic detail that seems to be used by Jesus for its literary emphasis and nothing more. Since the parable is concerned only with the present life, we cannot justly assume that these words of God represent a judgment after death. The expression, "Thou fool!" meant much more to the Jewish mind than a mere term of contempt. It was reserved for the impious and the atheistic, because the pious Jew, following the psalms, agreed that no greater folly existed than to rule God out of one's life. (Psalms 13 and 52 begin, "The fool says in his heart, 'There is no God.'")

Jesus Himself gives the lesson of the parable, that it is foolishness to be rich for oneself and not rich toward God. This moral, the warning against avarice, evidently had been prompted by the request of a man in the crowd who wished Jesus to decide on the legal question of a division of property. Without passing judgment on the licitness of the question, Jesus made it clear that He was not concerned with a temporality which in this case had proper legal procedure for its handling. He was, however, concerned with the need for avoiding an arrogant, greedy outlook.

Another lesson can be drawn from the parable; namely, that death can come upon us at any time. We must be ready to meet our God, with a record of a good life behind us.

THE BARREN FIG TREE

Lk. 13: 6–9

"A certain man had a fig-tree planted in his vineyard; and he came looking for fruit on it, and found none. So he said to the vine-dresser, 'See here! for three years I have come looking for fruit on this fig-tree, and have found none. Cut it down; why should it still encumber the ground?' But he answered him, 'Let it alone, sir, for this year too, until I dig about it and manure it. It may perhaps bear fruit after that; but if not, thou shalt cut it down.' "

Mt. 21:19–20

Seeing a fig-tree by the road-side He went up to it, and found nothing upon it but only leaves; and He said to it, *"Let no fruit ever again grow upon thee!"* And at once the fig-tree withered.

And seeing at some distance a fig-tree that had leaves He came up to see if He could find any fruit on it. On coming to it, however, He found nothing but leaves; for it was not the season for figs. Then, addressing it, He said, "Let no one ever again eat fruit from thee!" . . . And as they passed by in the morning they observed the fig-tree withered from its roots. And Peter, remembering, said to Him, "Rabbi, look! The fig-tree which Thou didst curse is withered."

Jesus often spoke of the danger of final impenitence, and in the context of the present parable reported by Luke, He had just reminded His listeners that physical calamities are not necessarily the result of great personal sin. None the less, He added, the temporal death such people suffered is the figure of the eternal death that results from sin. To illustrate this idea that our life on earth is a time of probation during which we are to bring forth spiritual good, He told the story of the unfruitful fig tree.

The parable as such is very simple. After three years of care a fig tree still remains sterile. Its owner accordingly orders that it be destroyed, but the vinedresser asks a reprieve for it, so that after more care it might become fruitful. If later it still fails, then it will be cut down.

Jesus seems to have intended that this parable would have meaning mainly for His Jewish audience. It seems more than coincidence, too, that He uttered it probably in the third year of His public life—and the owner of the fig tree says He has been looking for fruit for three years. This implies, then, that the willful rejection of the Messiah would lead to spiritual death. For the application to the individual, Jesus' earlier words give us the necessary clue, "Unless you repent, you shall all perish as well."

* * *

We should also consider here another fig-tree incident mentioned in Matthew and Mark. This is not so much a parable in word as a parable in action. The scene shifts from the unknown locale of Luke's account to the road between Bethany and Jerusalem. The time is no longer some day during the last year of Christ's apostolate, but is now early April, Monday of Holy Week, four days before Jesus died.

On this morning after Palm Sunday, Jesus was returning to Jerusalem from Bethany, and felt hungry. Seeing a fig tree by the roadside, He approached it to find nothing but leaves. With His next words, "Let no fruit ever grow again upon thee," the tree withered. Jesus took the occasion to say that powers of this sort and even more will be granted by God to those who have strong faith.

The difficulties of this event are numerous and call for careful explanation. To begin with, "it was not the season for figs," as Mark himself mentions; hence, the tree should not have borne fruit at the time. Could the incident be ascribed to childish petulance on Christ's part? Such an interpretation is wholly unworthy of anyone who believes in the divinity of Jesus. The sublime heights of moral perfection which Jesus everywhere manifested in His conduct contradict and prevent any such approach. None the less, if the fig tree could be taken to represent the Jewish people, who as a whole rejected the Messiah, how can this be a true parable in action since the tree could not fairly be expected to bear fruit at this spring season? Or if we were to think of the tree as if it had human characteristics, why should it have been condemned for following the laws of its Creator?

The answer must be sought from another quarter than that of our modern customs and outlook. Jesus adjusted Himself to the spirit of His times. Since He was always the great religious teacher, His listeners would see nothing incongruous in His adoption of some of the vigorous symbolic actions of the ancient prophets. Jeremiah had worn yokes on his neck to symbolize coming subjection; Isaiah had walked practically naked through the streets to indicate future distress; and Ezechiel had moved his possessions from the city to represent future calamities. Osee had married a harlot who later deserted him, and had given the children by this marriage symbolic names, all as a sign of the adulterous unfaithfulness of God's people.

We must not forget that the apostles were familiar with the concept of such biblical symbolism. Moreover, they had heard Jesus often enough speak of the fig tree as in Luke's parable. In justice to His undoubted sanctity, since His action could not be attributed to any shortcoming of irritability, the only logical conclusion would be its symbolic meaning.

We, too, arrive at this conclusion. Jesus took the enigmatic and paradoxical way of the prophets to show that the empty folly and hypocrisy of observing a law without a spirit was just so much empty foliage with no indication of the fruit that good works should have brought forth. God looks for this fruit in vain on this luxuriant tree, and must punish it accordingly. Again true to parabolic form, however, the detail of fruit being out of season was not part of the lesson which Jesus intended by His action. The empty foliage was sufficient for that.

At the moment, it is true, He referred only to the *power* of causing the fig tree to wither; strong faith would by God's aid do the equal of this and even more. But the true prophetic *symbolism* of His curse appeared in the parables He spoke to His disciples on the following days before His life came to its close. (See in this connection particularly the parables of the two sons and of the wicked tenants, pp. 97–103.)

THE BUDDING FIG TREE

Mt. 24:32–33

"Now learn from the fig-tree its lesson! When its branch now becomes tender, and puts forth its leaves, you know that summer is near. So you, also, when you see all these events, know that He is near, even at the doors."

Mk. 13:28–29

"Now learn from the fig-tree its lesson: When its branch is now become tender, and puts forth its leaves, you know the summer is near. So you also, when you see these events coming to pass, know that He is near, even at the doors."

Lk. 21:29–31

"Observe the fig-tree, and all the trees. When they are now budding forth, you see them and know of your own selves that summer is near. So you also, when you see these events coming to pass, know that the Kingdom of God is near."

Here Jesus calls attention to the annual reappearance of leaves on the fig tree. When the tree shows its life again each spring, it gives evidence that summer is soon to come. In the same way, when "these events" are seen, the disciples of Jesus should know that the Son of Man "is near, even at the doors."

This is an instance where the parable Jesus used is remarkably direct and simple in its own lesson, but the great difficulties arise from its context. The problem lies in deciding precisely what "these events" must be. It is the problem of what is called Christ's eschatological discourse. The word "eschatological" comes from the Greek *ta eschata* (pronounced es′-ka-ta), meaning "the last things." The discourse as such was given by Jesus to His disciples on some day in the early part of Holy Week, the last week of His life.

The explanation of the parable, it might seem, should not require a further discussion bringing in the enigmatic questions of the eschatological discourse. But the parable is followed by two sentences, "Indeed I tell you, this generation shall not pass away before all these things occur. Heaven and earth shall pass away, but My word shall not pass away." Are "these things" to be the signs of the coming of the Son of Man; namely, the cataclysmic upheavals in the heavens? If so, why did they not—or did they?—occur in the "generation" of Jesus, which was not to pass away until they were fulfilled? The application of the parable is denied if Jesus' words are not true. Hence, to explain this, the further explanation of the context is needed.

To summarize a very complicated and one of the most lengthy topics of gospel study, we must remember that the disciples first asked Jesus *two* distinct questions, which in their minds evidently were two aspects of the same event. "Tell us, when shall these things be?" (that is, the destruction of the temple at Jerusalem, as prophesied by Christ); and, "What shall be the sign of Thy coming and of the end of the world?" For the disciples the destruction of the temple would be equivalent to saying that the world had come to its end. The Messiah should then come in His glory to dispense final judgment.

Jesus' answer falls into distinct parts according to the two questions. In some cases we have little difficulty in recognizing what pertains to each part, and where. For example, tribulation for the apostles, the appearance of false prophets, the temple's profanation (the "abomination of desolation"), the haste to leave the city without stopping for belongings or clothes—these and similar details seem to hold true as signs of the impending capture of Jerusalem, as it did occur in A.D. 70. Jesus' further words that such tribulation "has not been since the beginning of the world until now, nor shall ever be," can be understood as prophetic hyperbole, a strong way of pointing out the suffering which would happen. They are not, in such an interpretation, taken as a strict comparison.

The second part of Jesus' discourse refers to the darkening of the sun and moon and the gathering of mankind by the angels (messengers) of the Son of Man. Even the phrase *"immediately after the affliction of those [earlier] days"* does not cause the difficulty it seems to have at first sight, for in such prophetical foreshortening everything is seen as happening at once. The interval between the fall of Jerusalem and the end of the world is passed over in silence.

The discourse as given in Matthew (24), Mark (13), and Luke (21) has often been outlined thus:

1. Signs of the fall of Jerusalem;
2. Signs of the end of the world;
3. Time of the fall of Jerusalem;
4. Time of the end of the world.

Thus, the phrase that "this generation will not pass away" would refer to the fall of Jerusalem. According to this meaning it was fulfilled, for "all these things" *concerning the fall of Jerusalem* were truly accomplished thirty-five years later, within the time specified by Jesus.

On the other hand, when Jesus added, "Of *that* day and hour, no one knows, not even the angels of heaven—none but the Father alone," He was referring to the second event, the end of the world. The knowledge of this is a mystery, reserved to God alone, unlike the warnings concerning Jerusalem which were truly utilized by the early Christians to their profit. They fled from the stricken city in time and thus escaped the holocaust and carnage that followed.

What of the phrase "Heaven and earth shall pass away"? This is merely a very vigorous and colorful Hebrewism. *"Even if Heaven, the abode of God, and earth, the abode of man, were to pass away, My word shall not do so."* In other words, the Hebrewism is a phrase put into the indicative mood as a certain future tense, whereas in modern English we would speak in a conditional subjunctive.

All this is admittedly an extremely compressed interpretation of Jesus' eschatological discourse, in so far as it is connected with the parable of the budding fig tree. So many are its complexities that entire books have been written on the subject. However, the key that unlocks most of the difficulties is this fact that two distinct events are discussed. The one, the fall of Jerusalem, is definite and clearly described as to time and circumstances. The other, the end of the world, is to come at a vague future date and is given in symbolic language.

JESUS THE GOOD SHEPHERD

Jn. 10:1–16

"Indeed, indeed, I say to you, he who does not enter the sheepfold by the door, but climbs in another way, that man is a thief and a robber; but he who enters by the door is shepherd of the sheep. To him the porter opens; and the sheep hearken to his voice, and he calls his own sheep by name, and leads them out. When he has brought out all his own sheep, he goes before them, and the sheep follow him because they know his voice. A stranger, however, they will not follow; on the contrary they run away from him, because they know not the voice of strangers." This allegory Jesus told them; but they did not understand what He was saying to them.

Jesus accordingly said to them again, "Indeed, indeed, I say to you, I am the Door for the sheep. All who came before Me are thieves and robbers; but the sheep did not hearken to them. I am the Door. If any one enters through Me, he shall be saved, and shall come in and go out, and find pasture. The thief comes only to steal and kill and destroy; I have come in order that they may have life, and may have it abundantly.

"I am the Good Shepherd. The good Shepherd lays down his life for his sheep. The hireling, who is neither shepherd nor owner of the sheep, on seeing the wolf coming leaves the sheep and takes to flight, and the wolf snatches and scatters them. He takes to flight because he is a hireling, and does not care for the sheep. I am the Good Shepherd, and I know My own, and My own know Me, as the Father knows Me, and I know the Father; and I lay down My life for My sheep. And other sheep I have which are not of this fold; those also I must bring, and they will hear My voice, and there shall be one flock under one Shepherd."

Mt. 26:31
And Jesus said to them, "You will all be scandalized over Me to-night; for it is written: I will 'smite the Shepherd, and the sheep of the flock shall be scattered.'"

Mt. 18:12–14
"If any man possesses a hundred sheep, and one of them wanders off, does he not leave the ninety-nine and go into the hills in search of the wanderer? And if he succeeds in finding it, indeed, I tell you that he rejoices over it more than over the ninety-nine which have not wandered away. Even so it is not the will of your Father who is in heaven that one of these little ones should perish."

Lk. 15:4–7
"What man among you who has a hundred sheep, and loses one of them, will not leave the ninety-nine in the desert, and go in search of the lost one until he finds it? And when he has found it he lays it on his shoulders rejoicing; and on coming home he calls his friends and neighbors together, saying to them, 'Congratulate me, for I have found my sheep that was lost!' So I tell

you there will be more gladness in heaven over one sinner who repents, than over ninety-nine righteous persons who need no repentance."

Most of the parables of Jesus are found in the synoptic gospels, with Matthew taking the lead in telling those with a doctrinal lesson and Luke first in the parables teaching a moral lesson that is so often one of mercy. John, however, presents the present long parable of the good shepherd which fits Jesus in so many details that it sometimes has been called an allegory. None the less, it correctly carries out the details of the Hebrew *mashal*, the story with a lesson.

The entire account reflects a charming picture of pastoral life in the Holy Land in the time of Jesus. The "sheepfold" was often no more than an enclosure of piled-up rocks, topped with brambles or thistles to keep out predatory animals. During the night the mixed flocks of sheep would be run into the fold by means of the one door. Another shepherd or hired man would watch these mixed flocks while their masters slept. Any man seen climbing into the sheepfold was automatically suspected of being a thief, for he would have been granted admission by the keeper of the gate if he were a lawful shepherd. In the morning each shepherd would claim his own animals to take them to pasture. The masters knew their own sheep, and the sheep themselves responded to their masters' calls, even the individual pet names they had been given. They would not, however, follow the voice of a stranger.

Since His disciples did not understand the application, Jesus Himself explained it. In a first tableau He is the door of the sheepfold; only through Him will the true pastures of eternal life be reached. The "thieves and robbers" who came before Him are probably the false teachers of the people who had made the Law a shambles of hypocritical observance.

Jesus changes the picture; He becomes no longer the door but now the good shepherd himself. Whereas the ordinary shepherd would not consider the preservation of the lives of his sheep as worth his own, this good shepherd would sacrifice even Himself to save His sheep from robbers. Nor would the hired man caring for the flock in the fold make this display of bravery against the wolves trying to snatch the sheep. (Jesus does not expatiate on who the "wolves" may be; perhaps this is a literary detail of the parable that is not necessary, although an application of it is easy to make!)

Again Jesus says He is the good shepherd, knowing His own in the same intimate way that God the Father knows Him and He knows the Father. He has other sheep which are not of His fold, the fold of the Chosen People. These are the gentiles whom He must also bring into His own flock, no longer the exclusive group of the Old Law but truly the universal Church of the New.

Sometimes the sentence "There will be one flock under one shepherd" has been taken as a divine prophecy that eventually the entire world will belong to Christ's Church. More likely, it does not seem to mean this much, for Jesus elsewhere foretold persecution and failure as the lot of His "little flock" (cf. Lk. 12:32). The statement apparently refers to the unifying influence of the new Church which will wipe out the exclusiveness of the old preparatory covenant.

In applying to Himself the title of "shepherd," Jesus could hardly have chosen a title more commonly applied to God in the Bible. The prophets and psalms had pictured God frequently as a shepherd leading His flock to green pastures. The only comparison that competes with it is the description of God and His people as husband and wife.

* * *

Jesus Himself at the time of His passion quoted the words of Zacharias, "I will 'smite the Shepherd, and the sheep of the flock shall be scattered.' " (Zach. 13:7 in Mt. 26:31). This sentence in itself is another compressed parable which Jesus is using to show that if the leader of the flock is destroyed, the unity of the flock is destroyed with him. We should notice, however, that the phrase does not hold true in the original prophecy in the same sense as Jesus later referred it to Himself. The "shepherd" in Zacharias is a false shepherd, a foolish shepherd who will lead his flock to ruin. Jesus certainly did not intend to take over this sense or meaning for Himself.

Instead, He used the quotation as one that would fit Him, but He changed its application from its original meaning to what is called an accommodation. It taught a new lesson, as every accommodated text of the Bible can do, but that lesson was no longer the meaning of the false shepherd of Zacharias. Jesus was the true shepherd of the flock, using the comparison even after His resurrection when He bestowed the primacy on Peter with the repeated words, "Feed My lambs, feed My sheep" (Jn. 21:16 ff.).

* * *

The image of Jesus as the good shepherd, taken from St. John's parable, has often been combined in art with the picture of another good shepherd in the parable of the lost sheep (Mt. 18:12–14; Lk. 15:4–7). Here Jesus speaks of a flock of a hundred sheep —a round number, not intended to express anything other than relative size—where one sheep has been lost. The stupidity of sheep is proverbial, and every shepherd knows that his livelihood depends on his ability to protect his sheep from the results of their own folly.

In this case the shepherd leaves the ninety-nine in a safe place while he searches for the one which has been lost. His rejoicing is so great as he carries the fatigued, perhaps wounded animal on his shoulders that he calls on his friends and neighbors to share his happiness.

The lesson of the parable is evidently this fact of proper joy over the return of a sinner to Christ's fold. That Jesus is the shepherd needs little proof; the difficulty occurs in our understanding of the phrase that "there will be more gladness in heaven over one sinner who repents than over ninety-nine righteous persons who need no repentance."

In context, when Jesus first uttered this parable, He evidently intended it to be a rebuke to the self-righteousness of the Pharisees and scribes, who, Luke tells us, murmured when they saw Jesus "receiving sinners and eating with them." We should, therefore, understand that the parable in no wise deprecates or minimizes the generosity of the just who persevere in the service of God. It is merely making its point, that the return of the sinner is desirable by all the members of the flock. When the flock becomes conscious of its own goodness to such an extent that it contemptuously looks down on a candidate for entrance, then it has lost its appreciation of goodness for the sake of goodness, and has substituted spiritual pride.

Without a doubt this expression comparing the joy over one sinner against that for the ninety-nine is just another example of Hebrew hyperbole. By means of a strongly worded statement the speaker makes it clear that he seriously intends his meaning. In this instance, for our instruction Jesus is emphasizing the joy in Heaven, where good abounds and only good can be desired. Therefore, Heaven's joy over the returned sinner should be imitated by the just on earth, who welcome him back to the fold.

Jesus' words, too, can remind us that our efforts for the kingdom of Christ must be for the common good of the kingdom. We must not have the selfish personal aim of gaining even the spiritual riches of so-called apostolic success achieved by ourselves.

THE LOST COIN

Lk. *15:8–10*

"What woman, possessing ten silver coins, if she loses one coin will not light a lamp and sweep the house, and search carefully until she finds it? And when she has found it, she calls her friends and neighbors together, saying, 'Congratulate me, for I have found the coin which I had lost!' So, I tell you, there is gladness in the presence of the angels of God over one sinner who repents."

This parable, coming as it does between that of the lost sheep and that of the prodigal son, is perfectly clear in its lesson. It is one more instance of Jesus' warm welcome for the repentant sinner, with an implied rebuke to the self-righteous among the scribes and Pharisees. The comparison this time is, of course, between the joy of the woman who has found her lost coin, and the joy of the angels over the sinner who has returned to God.

Some of the details connected with the parable have special interest. We have already mentioned Luke's predilection for those of the parables which centered around Christ's mercy and lovableness. But Luke has also won acclaim as the author of the "gospel of women." More than any other evangelist he has spoken of women and their interests. The present parable of the lost coin is so completely feminine in its details that we have reason to suspect it was reported to him by a woman in Jesus' audience—and who is a better candidate for this than Christ's mother, the undoubted source of so much other Lucan material?

It seems unfair to the housewife of the parable to accuse her of carelessness in losing the coin—a silver piece, the drachma, formerly valued at seventeen cents in American money. The story reads just as well if the loss is taken as an accident. Those scripture commentators who have upheld the "carelessness theory" have succeeded in showing a possible difference between the lessons of the parable of the lost sheep and the lost coin; but they may have done so more in the cause of male supremacy than that of gospel evidence, claiming that the sheep could have been lost only by accident but the coin by negligence.

More plausibly, we may rather say that this is the feminine counterpart of the parable of the lost sheep, the one applying to the male provider, the other to the female keeping house. Indeed, her conduct in "calling her friends and neighbors," as the shepherd did to tell them of his find, is even more true to life than the excitement pictured in the less emotional sex when his sheep was recovered. The value of the coin seems small, but in the circumstances it meant much to the housewife who could ill afford the loss, even though she still had nine coins like it. (As far as the parables themselves, her loss proportionately was much more than the one sheep: one-tenth instead of one-hundredth.) The masterful mind of the story-sermonizer saw this detail, teaching us that what we already possess seems to mean less to us than what we have lost.

One digression: It is very likely that this parable was responsible for our English idiom "to turn the house upside down" as an expression of careful searching. The Latin words for "sweeping the house" say *everrit domum*. Several manuscripts of the Latin Vulgate text mistook these words for *evertit domum*, "she turns over, upsets the house." Hence, some English translations in Bibles from Wyclif's time have said that the woman "turns the house upside down" in her anxiety to find the money.

THE PRODIGAL SON

Lk. 15:11–32

"A certain man had two sons, and the younger of them said to his father, 'Father, give me the portion of the property which falls to my share.' So he divided the property between them. Not many days after, the younger son, having collected everything, traveled to a distant land, and there squandered his fortune in voluptuous living. And when he had spent all, a terrible famine occurred in that country, and he himself began to be in want. So he went and engaged himself to one of the citizens of that country, who sent him upon his farm to feed swine. And he longed to fill his stomach with the carob-pods upon which the swine fed; and no one gave him anything.

"Coming then to himself he said, 'How many hired men in my father's service have bread enough and to spare, while I am perishing here with hunger! I will rise and go to my father, and will say to him, Father, I have sinned against heaven and in thy sight; I am no longer worthy to be called thy son; make me as one of thy hired men.' So he rose and returned to his father.

But while he was still a long way off, his father saw him, and was moved with pity; and running to meet him he fell upon his neck and kissed him. 'Father,' said the son to him, 'I have sinned against heaven and in thy sight; I am no longer worthy to be called thy son—' 'Be quick,' said the father to his slaves, 'and bring out the best garment, and clothe him in it; and put a ring on his finger, and sandals on his feet; and fetch the calf that we fattened, and kill it; and let us feast and have a merry time. For this son of mine was dead, and has come to life; he was lost, and is found!' They accordingly began to be merry.

"Now his elder son was out on the farm; and as he returned and drew near the house, he heard music and dancing. So calling one of the servants he asked what this meant. 'Thy brother has come,' he answered him, 'and thy father has killed the fattened calf, because he has him back safe and sound.' He was indignant, however, and refused to go in; so his father came out, and implored him. But in reply he said to his father, 'Look here! I have been slaving for thee so many years, and have never disobeyed a command of thine; yet thou hast never given me a kid, so that I might have a merry time with my friends! But as soon as this son of thine comes back, who has squandered thy property upon harlots, thou must kill for him the fattened calf!' 'Son,' he answered him, 'thou art always with me, and all that is mine is thine. But it was right that we should be merry and rejoice, because this brother of thine was dead and has come to life; he was lost and is found!' "

It seems almost sacrilegious to comment on a story which has been acclaimed for centuries as the masterpiece of all the masterpieces Jesus has left us in the parables. But while we admit that the telling of the story of the prodigal son cannot be improved upon, none the less there exist the usual obscurities and misunderstandings of a culture and a language far removed from our own times. The parable itself is so rich in meaning that its details can be studied almost endlessly, with our appreciation increasing proportionate to our study.

To begin with, the influence of this parable has led to a mistaken meaning of "prodigal," as if the word meant "repentant." Many people, thinking of the repentance of the son, do not perceive that his prodigality indicates how wasteful he was. A true prodigal is a spendthrift, not necessarily a great sinner, repentant or not.

A second misunderstanding concerns the main lesson of the parable. Is it the mercy of God toward the sinner, or, more probably, is it not a lesson for the self-righteous, not to condemn nor to be jealous of their brethren who have returned to God? The narrative does, indeed, have divisions corresponding to these ideas.

The first, as a setting, pictures the ingratitude of the sinner in misusing the gifts of his loving father. The second protests against harshness as it portrays the welcome which the merciful father gives the sorrowing son. The third is the mild but firm reproof administered by the father to the son who has never left him. Sketched in this fashion, the parable inevitably points to the need for human charity toward the fallen sinner rather than merely God's mercy toward him. Otherwise, the story would end midway, with the anticlimactic episode of the elder brother weakly tacked on as a sort of afterthought.

Still more reason exists for this conclusion when we note the context of Luke's gospel. His fifteenth chapter begins with the murmuring of the Pharisees and scribes because Jesus received and ate with sinners and publicans (the despised and incidentally unscrupulous tax collectors). The two parables that followed, of the lost sheep and lost coin respectively, each emphasized the value of the one repentant sinner *despite* the value of a majority of the just needing no serious repentance. These two accounts compared the values of restored animals and money with the value of a restored soul. Now the parable of the prodigal son compares the value in terms of a human being. But whereas the possible complaints of the apparently unrecognized just were left implicit in the first two, this third of the trilogy brings into the open a full discussion of the logic behind the original murmuring that was the occasion for all three parables.

We should note that not all the Pharisees were evil, even though the gospels condemn them in terms of their sect. We know explicitly of Nicodemus and of Joseph of Arimathea, good men and Pharisees. Many of the first Christians, too, were converted Pharisaic Jews. Accordingly, might we not extend the application of this parable of the prodigal son not merely to the malicious enemies of Christ, but perhaps even more so to the basically good among His listeners (and through them, we hope, to us), who needed (and need) its lesson?

As to details of the narrative, the portion of the estate for which the younger son asked must have been one-third. Jewish law (Deut. 21:17) gave the firstborn a double portion of the inheritance. In this case since there were two sons, the proportions would be in thirds. The "far country" to which the younger son now traveled in his foolishness is deliberately left vague, as a detail not necessary for the lesson of the parable. It was, however, a pagan land because of the swine we later learn were kept there. No Jew would dare raise an animal so impure according to the law.

The repentance of the boy seems genuine, once that hard experience has taught him the lesson of fair-weather friends who take advantage of his own stupid selfishness. He is willing to meet his father on any terms, so profound is his disgrace and his misery. (Jesus' choice of the swineherd occupation for the son, who did not have even the food given to the swine, was a masterful touch to bring home to the Jewish listeners the depths of this disgrace.)

We are struck by the fact that the father runs to meet the wastrel and gives him at once the kiss of welcome and peace. No wonder that this parable is so often called a pattern of God's mercy and love for us! The boy's confession is quickly made, down to its last humiliating detail. But the father calls for signs of honor to restore the prestige of the sinner. It is as if he had done nothing wrong, now that he has made his confession and thereby has promised amends. The mention of the fatted calf, incidentally, refers to a calf which was kept fattened so that it could be slaughtered on short notice and for special occasions such as this.

Jesus lets us have no doubts about the probity of the elder son. Not only did the heir stay faithful to the father when the younger son ran off to his license, but even now he "was out on the farm," and he was left unaware of the reason for the music and dancing at the very time he was laboring for his father.

It is completely possible that in actual life a doting father could be partial to the "baby" of the family, while unjustly failing to give the other children their due. Jesus has anticipated the objection in the parable. By showing the father's acceptance of the elder son's claims, Jesus makes it clear that the father is not unfair. It is rather a case of family unity looking toward the perfect welfare of *all* the members of the family rather than the selfish pitting of one against the other. We might say that Jesus is giving another example here of His lesson elsewhere expressed (as in the parable of the laborers in the vineyard). God's generosity to one of us does not take away God's generosity to another. Since *all* we have has come from the same Father, jealousy of this sort is simply against reason.

Up to the time of the father's quiet remonstrance, the elder son in the parable refuses to go in to the banquet for the prodigal. Then, still true to its nature of looking at only what it needs for its lesson, the story ends without letting us know the outcome— whether or not the elder son accepts his returned brother. That, however, is inconsequential. Jesus gained His purpose when He created His occasion to say, "It was right that we should be merry and rejoice, *because* this brother of thine was dead and has come to life; he was lost and is found."

THE SHREWD MANAGER

Lk. 16:1–9

"There was a certain rich man who had a manager, and this man was accused to him of wasting his property. So he called him up and said to him, 'What is this that I hear about thee? Hand in a statement of thy management; for thou canst be manager no longer.' 'Now what shall I do,' said the manager to himself, 'since my employer is taking the management from me? I am not strong enough to dig, I am ashamed to beg. I know what to do—so that, when I am removed from the management, people may receive me into their houses.' So inviting singly each of his employer's debtors, he asked the first, 'How much dost thou owe my employer?' 'A hundred kegs of oil,' he replied. 'Take thy bill,' he told him; 'sit down at once and write fifty.' Then he asked another, 'How much dost thou owe?' 'A hundred quarters of wheat,' was the answer. 'Take thy paper,' said he to him, 'and write eighty.' And his employer commended the defrauding manager, because he had acted cleverly; for the sons of this world are more clever in their own sphere than are the sons of the light. And I say to you, make for yourselves friends by means of the unrighteous mammon, so that, when it shall fail, they may receive you into the eternal dwellings."

No parable of Jesus has been the occasion for so much misunderstanding, confusion, and even expressed scandal as this story of the "shrewd manager." We have deliberately adopted this title in preference to other, older descriptions because it is suggested by the parable itself. Other titles, of course, have been the traditional "unjust steward" or the "unscrupulous," the "defrauding," the "unjust" manager. The very diversity of these names hints at the divergence of the interpretations. Some writers have gone so far as to say that the story should be passed over in silence because it is an occasion for scandal, as if Jesus were praising sinful conduct and holding it up for imitation. Others at the opposite extreme claim that no real difficulty exists if the purpose of the parable is kept in mind. The moderate view seems correct, in that the parable neither counsels worldly conduct nor does it make itself easily understood.

We do not know the occasion for the story. We do know that Jesus gave a strong lesson on the proper use of riches after he told of this manager. Evidently, it was to be a concrete introduction for later theory. At any rate, a rich owner of farmland discovered that his overseer had been wasting his property—how and when he learned of this the parable does not bother to indicate. Rhetorically, the owner calls for an accounting from his manager, but only as a way of making known his decision to dispense with his services. The manager implicitly admits his guilt by his acceptance of the verdict, and promptly begins to plan for a secure future now that his cozy livelihood is lost. He is not strong enough to dig for a living as a laborer; either his age or his dissipation or both have sapped his strength. For one who has had the prominence of such a position, begging would be the worst of humiliations. Hence, he plans a course of action which in a sense will be paid for by his present employer long after their connection has been severed.

He calls in the debtors. There has been some question whether these were men who actually owed money to the master, or whether they were the tenants on the large farm. The second answer is the likely one, for tenant farmers would ordinarily pay for their land in rent from its produce, not in money. The first tenant, therefore, owes a hundred barrels of oil; this is reduced by the manager to fifty. We must remember that he still has the authority to make a decision of this sort in the name of his master. The second debtor owes some fourteen hundred bushels of wheat. Since this amount is so large, the manager reduces it by only one-fifth.

Now comes the conclusion of the parable, controversial and distressing to some, but, we repeat, perfectly understandable in the light of the comparison Jesus planned to make. Some translations have said that "the lord commended the defrauding manager." This "lord" should never have been interpreted as God. He is merely the employer, and he is as worldly minded as his employee. He commended him, we note, because he acted not so much "wisely" (and certainly not "justly"!), but in the root sense of the gospel words, he acted *shrewdly* and *cleverly*. The owner wryly discerned a touch of humor in the rascal's conduct. To the

74

very end he remained a self-seeking albeit clever knave, and the owner felt that he deserved credit accordingly.

The manager had certainly been unjust to begin with. The added question is, Was he unjust in his reduction of the amounts due his employer? Various answers are possible. We have already mentioned that in virtue of the authority with which the master had entrusted him he could make such dispositions of the property as he saw fit. Another answer is that such conduct merely continued the absconding that had previously occurred.

A third answer, relatively unknown to the lay reader, is based on the existence of graft in all such renting operations. Under terms of leasing and even subleasing, each new grant would be the occasion for an extra taxation. The top owner would be aware of such goings on, but would be content with getting what he felt was his due, and would permit his underlings to gouge others down the line without any particular scruple on his part. Applied to the present case, this would mean that the manager had overcharged the tenants for rent from the beginning. When he reduced the prices he demanded of them, he was merely asking for the just price he should have asked in the first place, as due his owner. The amount he remitted was his "forgiving" the amount of the graft or bribe originally intended for his own purse!

An interpretation such as this not only agrees with customs of the times, but also fits the final lesson of the parable. The owner's commendation of the manager shows that the owner was as worldly minded as his steward. He recognized, therefore, that while the manager succeeded in clearing up his accounts, he did it in such a way as to make friends in the process. He gave up merely what had never been his in the first place.

Now for the comparison made by Jesus. His words are, "The sons of this world are more clever in their own sphere than are the sons of light." The comparison is between the effort and intelligence shown in a *worldly* cause and the efforts and intelligence shown in a *spiritual* cause. It is critically important to note that *Jesus* did *not* praise the shrewd manager; the worldly owner did. Nor should we say that Jesus' words hint that good people can never make an honest, prosperous living in business. Such a claim mixes the comparisons.

Jesus is simply pointing out the greater cleverness developed in people by the prospect of temporal gain, compared to the lesser intelligence displayed by people whose prospect of spiritual gain thereby enamors them less. Jesus never hints in the slightest that the conduct of the manager should be imitated. However, the way in which he devotes his talents to a wasted cause is reason enough to shame good people who have an eternally worth-while cause but do not work for it.

*　　*　　*

The next sentence, verse 9 in Luke, ordinarily included in this parable, is the following: "And I say to you, make for yourselves friends by means of the unrighteous mammon, so that, when it shall fail, they may receive you into the eternal dwellings." As if this sentence were not confusing enough in exact translation from the Greek, an older English version reads, "Make unto you friends of the mammon of iniquity, that when *you* shall fail, they may receive you into everlasting dwellings."

The first question to decide is whether this is the concluding application which according to Jesus is to fit within the parable, or whether He used it to introduce the next development of His thought, namely, the proper use of money. Where learned scholars hesitate to give a final decision, we certainly do not intend to take such a step here. None the less, we believe that the sentence is understood more easily if it is divorced from the preceding parable. Luke's verses 10 through 13 drive home the idea that God and mammon (the Aramaic word for money) cannot be both served. Verse 9 accordingly can be paraphrased, "I tell you very seriously that you should make *true* friends for yourselves, friends therefore in the spiritual order; and do this *by means* of this very money, which has been called unrighteous mammon and filthy lucre. Use your money wisely for eternal things (such as giving alms to the poor), so that when it, your money, fails, these true friends you have gained shall receive you into eternal dwellings."

If, however, one wishes to read this sentence in connection with the parable, then the meaning would be, "Just as the shrewd manager made friends for himself by means of money, which is so often called unrighteous money because of its misuse, so should you make true, spiritual friends for yourselves by proper use of this oft misused medium, so that these true friends shall receive you into eternal dwellings.

According to either approach, in the translation of Father Kleist, "Money is a worthless thing; but use it to make friends for yourselves, so that when it gives out, they may receive you in the everlasting homes."

A SLAVE OF TWO MASTERS?

Lk. 16:10–13

"He who is faithful in a very little thing is also faithful in much; and he who is unjust in a very little thing is also unjust in much. If therefore you have been unfaithful with regard to the unrighteous mammon, who will entrust you with true riches? And if you have been unfaithful with regard to what belongs to another, who will give you what is your own? No servant in a household can serve two masters; for either he will hate the one and love the other, or he will devote himself to one and despise the other. You cannot serve God and mammon."

"No man can serve two masters; for either he will hate the one and love the other, or he will be devoted to the one and despise the other. You cannot serve God and mammon."

This compressed parable is more of a proverb than a story, although the form in which Luke presents it is somewhat longer than that in Matthew. Luke quotes Jesus as saying, "No servant in a household (that is, no slave) can serve two masters." Matthew carries the phrase merely as, "No man can serve two masters."

This divergence between the two evangelists does not necessarily mean that one of them has changed the parable from its original context. It is practically certain that Jesus repeated the same sayings at different periods of His public life. None the less, in finding it as part of the Sermon on the Mount in Matthew, we should remember Matthew's tendency to group his material according to topic rather than to chronology. We know that all the contents of the Sermon on the Mount were not actually proposed by Jesus at one time.

Luke placed the parable directly after the conclusion about the shrewd manager. As we already mentioned, the reference in verse 9 on making friends of mammon may well be the introduction to the present teaching of Jesus on the well ordered use of money.

The possible misunderstandings of the parable are removed by grasping the connotation of our English word "servant." In the gospel this has been translated from the Greek idea of "slave." Therefore, since a slave belongs *completely* to his master, it is impossible for two men to own one slave and simultaneously to claim his full allegiance. Still more reason will exist for this impossibility when, as Jesus implies, there is violent enmity between the two masters.

The remaining source of confusion for twentieth century readers is Christ's use of "mammon." This is (as we earlier indicated) an Aramaic word, transliterated into English and translated as "money." We should keep in mind that "mammon" of itself has neither a good nor a bad connotation. The context where it is used alone indicates that. But by the fact that Jesus places "mammon" opposite "God," and "unrighteous mammon" opposite "true riches," He evidently is thinking of money as a source of inordinate attachment, and to that extent, in a poor sense.

With these explanations, certain false interpretations of the parable immediately stand out as ridiculous. Such a one would be the opinion that Jesus denied the possibility for a modern worker to hold two positions at the same time, or that Jesus condemned *all* possession of money, no matter how detached the owner might be from it so that he would neither hoard it nor spend it inordinately.

THE RICH GLUTTON AND LAZARUS

Lk. 16:19–31

"There was once a certain rich man, who was clothed in purple and fine linen, and daily lived in feasting and splendor. And a certain beggar named Lazarus was laid at his gate covered with sores, and longing to be fed with the scraps dropped from the rich man's table. Even the dogs came and licked his sores.

"By and by, however, the beggar died, and was conveyed away by the angels into Abraham's bosom. The rich man also died and was buried; and in the abode of the dead he raised his eyes, while in the midst of torment, and saw Abraham afar off, and Lazarus in his bosom. Then shrieking out he cried, 'Father Abraham, have pity on me, and send Lazarus to dip the tip of his finger in water and cool my tongue; for I am tortured in this flame!' 'Child,' replied Abraham, 'remember that thou didst receive thy good things in thy lifetime, just as Lazarus received evils; so now he is consoled here, while thou art in anguish. And besides all this, there is immovably fixed between us and you a vast abyss, so that those who wish to pass from us to you may not be able, and that none may cross over from you to us.'

" 'Then I implore thee, Father,' said he, 'to send him to my father's house—for I have five brothers—to give them solemn warning, so that they too may not come into this place of torment.' 'They have Moses and the Prophets,' replied Abraham; 'let them listen to them.' 'Ah, no, Father Abraham!' was his answer; 'but if some one goes to them from the dead they will repent.' 'If they will not listen to Moses and the prophets,' came the reply, 'neither would they believe were one to rise from the dead.' "

This parable is popularly known as "Dives and Lazarus." The word *dives* means "rich" in Latin. Hence, it was applied to the rich man of the parable as his proper name, although he is actually anonymous. "Lazarus" was a name not uncommon among the Jews, and the beggar here is not to be confused with the Lazarus who in real life was the brother of Mary and Martha at Bethany in the family of friends of Jesus.

One other caution: All the qualities of imaginary dialogue expected in a parable for their teaching value also appear here. Therefore, we do not favor the opinion that the rich man was a living person instead of merely a type; or that Jesus is actually revealing the damnation and salvation of the rich man and Lazarus respectively.

Purple garments and fine linen were restricted to the wealthy. The mention of them in the parable indicates the opulence which was manifestly exhibited in the sinful, luxurious banquets. Lazarus was so poor and so helpless that even the dogs licked his ulcerous sores. For a Jewish listener this gave a concrete picture of his utter misery.

When Jesus says that the angels carried the beggar into Abraham's bosom, He does not intend to teach exact details of the afterlife. It is evident that He describes Heaven in terms which His listeners would understand: a happiness of reclining with Abraham on his bosom or in his lap. The rich man is described in torment after his death. Here we must particularly caution against a pernicious misunderstanding. The rich man cries out with remorse and sorrow and some evident good will in trying to help at least his brothers on earth from reaching the abyss of punishment to which he has been assigned. In this respect such is *not* a picture of hell. No soul in hell, no wicked angel, could ever begin to entertain sentiments such as these. The damned hate God implacably, and they hate all that is good with the same fixed hate. Since their will is set in evil by their own unchangeable decision, any comparison between them and the rich man is, in this aspect of the parable, completely out of place.

The first lesson of the parable is evidently the need to live properly in this life as a prelude to happiness in the next. The second lesson is that the means God gives us on earth to save our souls are truly sufficient. We do not need "some one from the dead" to incite us to generosity or to instruct us to truth. In the words Jesus put into Abraham's mouth, if the rich man's five brothers will not listen to Moses and the prophets (that is, the two great divisions of the Jewish scriptures, the Law and the Prophets), then they will not have enough good will to obey the word of someone come from the afterlife.

It would be a misinterpretation of the parable to use it as an invective against riches as such. Equally wrong would be the claim that poverty as such is holy and good. Riches and poverty are neither good nor bad of themselves. Their acceptance in accordance with God's law, and God's will is what is important. This is the third lesson, equivalently, that worldly prominence as such

does not save one's soul. The fourth and perhaps even most prominent lesson is the fact that the rich man could have saved his soul
by using superfluous wealth in giving alms to Lazarus.

Verse 23 carries the sentence that the rich man "in hell raised
his eyes" to Abraham. In Jesus' time Jewish belief concerning
the nature of the afterlife was vague. Hell (*Hades* in Greek,
Sheol in Hebrew), was merely the abode of the dead. It comprised
two regions: Gehenna, for the wicked, and Paradise, or place of
rest, for the just. Between them was an impassable abyss. The
concept, therefore, was still incomplete, and as such it was accommodated and tolerated by Jesus as the backdrop of the parable.
Of interest to us is the derivation of "Gehenna" from the name
of the valley of "Ge-Hinnom." This was south of Jerusalem. In
ancient times, so it was said, infants had been sacrificed there to
the god Moloch. The Jews held it in horror as a place of abomination, and used it as a garbage dump where fires were kept con-
stantly burning. It is easy to discern the parallel, whereby this
valley would symbolize hell and give its name to it as "Gehenna."

THE GODLESS JUDGE

Lk. 18:1–8

He also told them a parable, to the effect that they ought to
pray at all times and not grow faint-hearted.

"There was a judge," said He, "in a certain town, who neither
feared God nor had regard for man. And there was a widow in
that town who kept coming to him, saying, 'Give me judgment
against my adversary.' He would not, however, for a while; but
afterward he said to himself. 'Although I neither fear God nor
have any regard for man, yet, because this widow is troublesome

to me, I will give judgment in her favor, or she will have me worn out with her incessant visits.'

"Hear now," the Lord added, "what this unjust judge says. And will not God avenge His elect, who cry to Him day and night, and will He delay long over their case? I tell you, He will avenge them speedily. However, when the Son of Man comes, will He find faith on the earth?"

The lesson of this parable of the godless judge is clearly stated in Luke, "that they ought to pray at all times and not grow faint-hearted." The character of the judge is painted in very poor colors. He has evidently fallen away from all religious ideals, "not fearing God," and is so ruthless that he does not "fear man." He also must have been a minor official, for in a major Jewish court the justice would have been administered not by one man but by a tribunal. At any rate, unscrupulous and hardhearted as he is, he finally listens to a helpless widow's plea for redress against her oppressor simply because she will otherwise wear him out by her incessant visits.

The word translated here as "wear out" means literally "to strike in the face," but it seems justifiable to take it in a metaphorical sense. The widow, already so oppressed because she lacks a husband to defend her, would hardly be able to do the judge physical violence.

If, then, a man so heartless can be brought to change his mind, how much more will not the all-loving Father hear the prayers of His "elect," that is, His chosen ones. But this does not mean that a multitude of prayers might irritate God, as it were, to grant any petition, no matter how bad for us. The parable merely applies to the comparative results obtained from persevering prayer.

There is no absolute agreement among scripture commentators on the exact meaning of the sentence, "When the Son of Man comes, will He find faith on the earth?" It seems more likely that this phrase does not belong to the parable as a conclusion. There-fore, a corresponding interpretation should not be forced out of it. As a rhetorical question, it would seem to imply that when Jesus does come in His glory at the end of the world, lively faith will have failed many.

Whether the entire parable of the unjust judge is to be ap-plied to perseverance up to and including the end of the world, or whether it is merely a general exhortation to be steadfast in prayer is also a point that can be argued both ways. The "praying at all times" which is the explicit lesson does not mean the literal re-peated utterance of prayers, but rather the frame of mind which would utilize all possible occasions for prayer. It must be under-stood according to reason. Otherwise, literally "to pray always" would lead to a neglect of the duties of one's state of life and fail-ure to take proper care of one's health. To that extent, it would be against God's expressed will. In all our conduct moderation should reign.

THE PHARISEE AND THE PUBLICAN

Lk. 18:9–14

He told this parable also to some who were confident of their own righteousness, and despised all others: "Two men went up to the temple to pray, the one a Pharisee, the other a publican. The Pharisee stood and prayed thus about himself: 'O God, I thank Thee that I am not like the rest of men—extortioners, unjust, adult-erers—or even like this publican. I fast twice in the week. I give tithes of all my income!' But the publican, standing far off, would not so much as raise his eyes to heaven, but smote his breast, say-ing, 'O God, be merciful to me the sinner!'

"This man, I tell you, went back to his house justified rather than the other. For every one who exalts himself shall be humiliated; but he that humbles himself shall be exalted."

This is the well known story of the Pharisee and the publican who went to the temple to pray. The Pharisee vaunted his goodness, but the publican humbly admitted his sinfulness. The prayer of humility was accepted by God in a way far superior to the prayer of self-righteousness.

Commentators have argued rather strongly as to the precise lesson of the parable. Some have suggested it as a lesson in the proper attitude for prayer. Others maintain it is a lesson of humility. Actually, the two lessons merge into one although it would appear that Jesus wished to inculcate humility first, no matter what other moral the parable was to impart. The reason for this opinion lies in the words of Luke, "He told this parable to some who were confident of their own righteousness and despised all others." This seems to be so clear a description of the attitude of the Pharisees that we cannot doubt the target of the story.

Sometimes the readers of the gospel get the impression that Jesus condemned all Pharisees in every way. Such an idea is not fully correct. Jesus spoke against an observance of the law down to the smallest letter wherein all the *spirit* of the observance had been lost. We must not think that His condemnation of this formalism is identical with a reprobation of all ceremony and external minutiae. The external observance can be genuine only if and when it is based on a genuine internal spirit. On the other hand, the internal spirit must be judged spurious if it does not symbolize and manifest itself by some external action.

Sometimes the Pharisee in the parable has been criticized for his pride in praying while standing. In absolute fact this posture cannot be judged as unduly bold, for it was a common Jewish posture for prayer. Moreover, it is striking that the parable does not in so many words *condemn* the Pharisee for what he has done.

The good deeds he recites are truly far more than was required. Jesus does not blame him for this. It is the implicit *attitude* of the prayer which is at fault; namely, a reminder to God of the individual virtues, self-centered instead of God-centered.

The ordinary translation, "This man went back to his house justified *rather than* the other," does not completely express the meaning of the Aramaic original. As Jesus spoke the words, He had to use a form of comparison which the Greek translation followed quite literally. But in doing this, it betrays the first meaning in the Aramaic: "This man went back to his house justified *more than* the other." Jesus does not dispute the fact that in the sight of the law the Pharisee is "justified"—made holy—by his punctilious works. His justification, however, remains as legal after his prayer as it was beforehand.

The parable ends with a proverbial comment which again affords occasion for conflicting interpretations. "Every one who exalts himself shall be humiliated; but he that humbles himself shall be exalted." Does this phrase belong to the parable as an integral conclusion, extending the lesson, or is it a sort of appendix that adds to the parable while independent of it? Arguments exist in both directions.

On the one hand, the publican seems to have been exalted in God's eyes by his humility, but where and how has the Pharisee been humiliated and lowered? Especially if he is merely *less* justified than the publican? On the other hand, the relative meaning of this aphorism certainly holds true. Compared to each other, the publican and Pharisee were treated differently by God. He who thought himself spiritually higher was considered actually less; and he who lowered himself in God's sight was given greater spiritual credit for doing so.

Jesus' master stroke in this parable is His choice of the publican as the counterfoil of the Pharisee. As far as public appearances or opinion were concerned, the publican was a renegade Jew, hired by the hated Romans as a sort of representative. We must remember that taxes were farmed out to a highest bidder, who paid the ruling power what it thought it should obtain, and then proceeded to recoup his expenses—with ample profit—by gouging the common folk for all he could get. The publican was justly loathed for the unjust extortions he committed. Yet, in the parable, he is pitted against the Pharisee, the very personification of the full external observance of the Jewish law.

Jesus never justified the thievery of the tax gatherers. When, however, they were repentant and wished to make amends, they were received warmly by the Lord. In the present parable one of their profession was privileged to be chosen as a type and symbol of true, prayerful humility.

THE CAPRICIOUS CHILDREN

Lk. 7:31–35

"To what, therefore, shall I compare the men of this generation, and what are they like? They are like children sitting in the market-place, shouting to one another and saying, 'We piped for you, and you did not dance; we wailed, and you did not weep.' For John the Baptizer has come neither eating bread nor drinking wine; and you say, 'He has a demon!' The Son of Man has come eating and drinking; and you say, 'Look at Him! a man who is a glutton and a wine-guzzler! a friend of publicans and sinners!' Yet wisdom is justified by all her children."

Mt. 11:16–19

"But to what shall I compare this generation? It is like children sitting in the market-places and shouting to their playmates, 'We piped for you, and you did not dance; we wailed, and you did not mourn.' For John came neither eating nor drinking; and they say,

'He has a demon!' The Son of Man has come eating and drinking; and they say, 'Look at Him! a man who is a glutton and a wine-guzzler! a friend of publicans and sinners!' Yet Wisdom is justified by her works."

Jesus had just finished praising the great holiness manifested by John the Baptist in his vocation as forerunner of the Messiah. Implicitly, He indicated that John had come to announce Him, and John had been refused by the Pharisees just as Jesus was now being refused. In this context, then, Jesus told the parable of the children in the market place.

These children have sometimes been called "stubborn" or "wayward." Since the parable shows how often they change their mind, they should rather be called "capricious." In other words, not knowing what they wanted, they were never satisfied and would complain no matter what was done for them. In this respect they anticipated the conduct of the Pharisees. John the Baptist's austerity had drawn from the Pharisees the sarcastic accusation that he was diabolically possessed, simply because he was so austere. On the other hand, when Jesus, mixing with the people, accepted the amenities of everyday life in food and drink, the Pharisees shifted their attack and called Him a glutton and guzzler of wine.

The games of the children in the parable were the mimicking of adults in the joyous celebration of a wedding or the loud lamentation at a funeral. It is not clear whether Jesus wished to picture two groups disagreeing on the type of game to play, wedding or funeral; or whether one group of children tries to please others, all to no avail, no matter what game they try. The nature of the parable does not mean that each, the "dancers" of the wedding game and the "wailers" of the funeral game, represents Jesus and John. None the less, the contrast between the warmth of Jesus and the severity of John is hinted at.

The story ends with a sentence often obscure to many people. "Yet wisdom is justified by all *her children*" (as in Luke), or "by *her works*" (as in the Greek manuscripts of Matthew). Two interpretations are possible. First, not all these people who heard John and Jesus rejected them with capricious reasoning, as did the Pharisees. The true believers thus vindicated ("justified") wisdom by their conduct as her children.

As a more likely interpretation, the message of salvation is to be transmitted in two different ways, that is, by the strictness of John and the mildness of Jesus. It has been vindicated in this plan to appeal to different people in different ways, for the bad will of its opponents has appeared in the self-contradictory pretexts they used to reject it.

THE MERCILESS DEBTOR

Mt. 18:23–35

"The Kingdom of Heaven, therefore, may be compared to a king who desired to settle accounts with his servants. And when he had begun to settle accounts, one was brought to him who owed him ten thousand talents. And as he had no means of refunding, his master gave orders that he should be sold, together with his wife and children and everything he had, and the amount paid up. That servant, therefore, fell prostrate before him, crying, 'Have patience with me, and I will repay thee all!' And the lord of that servant, moved with compassion, released him and remitted to him the debt. That same servant, however, on going out, met one of his fellow-servants who owed him a hundred denarii; and he seized him by the throat, crying, 'Pay what thou owest!' His fellow-servant, therefore, fell down and implored him, saying, 'Have patience with me, and I will repay thee!' He would not, however, but went and threw him into prison until he should repay the debt. When his fellow-servants saw what had occurred, they were deeply grieved, and went and detailed to their lord all that had happened. Then his lord, sending for him, said to him, 'Thou villainous slave! I remitted to thee the whole of thy debt because thou didst entreat me; shouldst thou not also have had pity on thy fellow-servant, just as I had pity on thee?' And his enraged master handed him over to the jailers, until he should pay the entire debt. So, too, will My heavenly Father do to you, if you do not, every one of you, forgive your brother from your hearts."

As a lesson in fraternal charity and forgiveness of one's neighbor, this parable is one of the easiest to understand. The kingdom of Heaven is not directly compared to the king settling accounts with one of his officials. Instead, Jesus' meaning is that such a situation can well occur in the organization or Church Jesus is founding on this earth. The official's debt of ten thousand talents is at the minimum ten million dollars in modern currency without considering the effects of modern inflation. This huge sum is not out of keeping with reality even though it appears in a parable. The minor officials of an oriental despot might well run up so tremendous a debt through luxurious living. The procedure for handling a bad debt is about to be applied in this case, namely, the sale of the debtor as well as his wife and children as slaves. Moved to compassion by his abject pleas, the king forgives him the money he owes.

The erstwhile debtor, however, has not learned the lesson of mercy which was applied to him in his own favor. He violently throttles a fellow official who owes him a hundred denarii—some seventeen dollars, about 1/600,000th of the sum forgiven him by the king. His hardheartedness extends to demanding a jail sentence until the hundred denarii are paid. The king, of course, hears of the action, and in a rage hands him over to the jailers until he pays his entire first debt.

Incidentally, Jesus refers to the "jailers" with a word that carries the meaning of "torturers," a meaning related to the punishments of the afterlife which Jesus describes. In this way He hints at the lesson of the parable, the punishment of God on those who are unmerciful.

The final sentence must be understood in context and with proper applications of supernatural prudence: "So, too, will My heavenly Father do to you, if you do not, every one of you, forgive your brother from your hearts." The general lesson is clear, that our sins make us debtors of God to an extent far greater than can occur in our dealings with our fellow men and women who perchance may offend us; hence, our mercy must extend just as bounteously to them.

The details of the parable do not apply. Thus, for instance, God does not demand our service and obedience to His law in some sort of mercenary way which He would require in order for Himself to stay in existence. Moreover, even if and when we commit the sin of unmercifulness toward our neighbor, God offers His mercy to us as long as we are in this life and are willing to repent of our evildoing. Finally, the law of Christian charity does not mean that we must close our eyes to the fact of open hatred or aggression. The duties of our state of life and our responsibilities to those who depend on us may well require a strong defense of our rights.

This is fully in accord with Christ's law of mercy, provided we do not act in a spirit of vengeance but use forceful action only in so far as is necessary according to the virtue of justice. As the parable so sharply teaches, we must be ready to forgive our neighbor's faults and offenses especially when he repents of them and asks our mercy. In the case of continued enmity our Christian mercy will seek all possible means of excusing his conduct on the score of extenuating circumstances known only to God.

THE LABORERS IN THE VINEYARD

Mt. 19:30; 20:1–16

"But many shall be last who are first, and first who are last. For the Kingdom of Heaven is like a householder, who went out in the early morning to hire laborers for his vineyard. And having agreed with the laborers for a denarius a day, he sent them into his vineyard. And he went out about nine o'clock and saw others standing idle in the market-place; and he said to these, 'You also go into my vineyard, and I will pay you whatever is just.' They accordingly went. And going out again about noon, and about three o'clock, he did the same. But about five o'clock he went out and found others standing; and he said to them, 'Why do you stand here all day idle?' 'Because,' they said to him, 'no one has hired us.' He said to them, 'Go you also into the vineyard.' When evening came, the owner of the vineyard said to his overseer, 'Call the laborers and pay them their wages, beginning with the last up to the first.' And when those who went in about five o'clock came up, they each received a denarius. So when the earliest hired came up, they concluded that they were to receive more; but they, too, received each a denarius. And on receiving it they grumbled against the master, saying, 'These last comers did but one hour's work; yet thou hast put them on an equal footing with us, who have borne the day's burden and the scorching heat!' 'My good fellow,' he answered one of them, 'I am doing thee no wrong; didst thou not engage with me for a denarius? Take what is thine and go. It is my will to give as much to this last comer as to thee. Am I not allowed to do what I like with my own? Hast thou an envious eye because I am generous?' Thus the last shall be first and the first last; [for many are called, but few are chosen.]"

On several scores this parable has been the occasion for perplexed and sometimes contradictory interpretation. Difficulties have arisen from the questions of how far Jesus wished the details of the parable to apply for its lesson, and whether or not the concluding sentence is an integral part of the parable and is to be interpreted accordingly. This is the well known paradox, "The last shall be first, and the first last, for many are called but few are chosen."

The story begins logically in its context. A rich young man who wished to live a more perfect life found himself unwilling to give up his wealth completely in order to follow Jesus. Peter spoke up in his own name as well as for the other apostles, and asked Jesus what would be the lot of Christ's followers. Jesus promised the hundredfold in return and life everlasting, and added, "But many shall be last who are first, and first who are last." In other words those who are last according to worldly standards can become first in spiritual wealth if they so wish; and those who are wedded to wealth will lose their apparent "first" position and become last in actuality. Then Jesus began the parable of the laborers in the vineyard to exemplify what He had just said. "*For* the Kingdom of Heaven is like a householder, who went out in the early morning to hire laborers for his vineyard.

We are accustomed to this type of introductory phrase in Jesus' parables, not meaning, of course, that the kingdom of God *is* the householder, but that a comparison will be made between the situation of the parable and that which exists in the Church of Christ, the kingdom of God.

The parable in many respects is extremely true to life. According to custom the owner of the vineyard goes out in the early morning to hire his men for the day. The "denarius" he offers them is the just wage for a day's work. It is considered reasonable and to that extent generous. Later in the day, at nine, twelve, and three o'clock, he finds others standing idle in the market place, where men looking for work would logically congregate. He offers them no longer the standard pay for one day but changes the offer to "what is just." At five o'clock he finds still others waiting around, and learns that they are there because no one yet has hired them. This time he makes no offer as to the pay they shall receive, but merely sends them into his vineyard.

The time schedule followed in the parable is calculated according to the method which the Jews had adopted from the Romans. The night was divided into four watches of three hours apiece, beginning at six in the evening, or about dusk. The day was divided correspondingly into four hours, named after the one of the twelve hours which immediately preceded it. Thus, beginning at six in the morning, or dawn, nine o'clock would be the third hour; noon, the sixth; three o'clock, the ninth. The "eleventh hour" of the parable came directly before evening set in at six, with the first watch of the night. It is this reference in the parable which is the source for our "eleventh hour" phrase in modern English as a description of last-minute action.

None the less, despite all these agreements with reality Jesus took advantage of the typical freedom of the Hebrew parable in order to build up His story for its lesson. If the householder needed laborers, why did he not hire all these men at once, instead of waiting later in the day, when they would say they had no one to hire them? This discrepancy with everyday experience appears sharpest in the case of the men of the eleventh hour. The answer, of course, is that Jesus wished to create a situation where men who worked in unequal amounts would receive equal pay. In line with this aim He also arranged that the last should be paid first so that the apparent inequality of pay would be noticed, and to that extent the introductory phrase would be justified, "The last shall be first."

Various lessons have been drawn from this parable, but the main lesson is the freedom of God to use His gifts as He wills. The thought behind the narrative goes back to the reversal of status brought about by possessing the spiritual riches of following Christ instead of adhering to temporal wealth alone. God, then, is free in distributing such gifts to those who have renounced all to follow Him in His kingdom.

Moreover, these generous promises are made to all who enter the kingdom, whether they come early or late, but provided only that they *come*. The lesson here is akin to that of the parable of the prodigal son. Those who have been faithful to God have worked in the vineyard long and arduously. Sinners who have been converted to Him have arrived there but recently. None the less, those He has received first must not be jealous and resentful because He has extended to others the generosity which they had first received. If there was any immediate reference at all on the day Jesus spoke this parable, it must have been the implication that the spiritually proud Pharisees were the workers of the first hour who looked down on the sinners coming after them who were warmly received by Jesus.

Throughout all Christian centuries other lessons, too, have been proposed. For instance, the laborers of the first hour have been interpreted as the Jews, those of the eleventh hour as the gentiles. Again, the various hours have been taken to mean the various ages of the world when different peoples are called to follow Christ. These hours are also the call of Jesus, it is said, which comes to some people early in life, to others in succeeding years until just before death. Despite this suggested interpretation the parable should not be thought of as describing the day of life which ends in death. In other words, death does not occur after the eleventh hour; the question rather concerns the entrance into Christ's kingdom and the acceptance thereby of the organization Jesus established on earth wherein the will of God would be ideally fulfilled.

There is one implication which should be branded completely false. Such is the idea that since Christ, the owner of the vineyard, contracted with each man for what He thought just and for what the man accepted, therefore, any modern employer would be justified in giving even sweatshop wages, provided the penury of his workmen forced them to accept any offer. This wrong view would be equally reprehensible when appearing in the form of a supposed concession to workmen to charge for their labor (or to merchants to charge for their goods) "all that the trade can bear," against the principles of social justice. The reason for discarding these false views of the parable is the fact that the denarius was a just and generous and commonly accepted day's wage.

We mentioned earlier that the concluding paradoxes of the parable have caused much speculation as to their real purport. As far as concerns "Many are called but few are chosen," we prefer to accept the opinion of many scholars that this phrase does not belong here, and that it was misplaced by reason of a copying error or other misunderstanding. It occurs rightly and originally at the end of the parable of the wedding feast (Mt. 22:14), and we shall discuss it later in that connection. (See page 112.)

The other phrase, "The last shall be first and the first last," has also come in for its share of varying interpretations. Some writers have considered it as a sort of proverb which does not have a direct connection with the parable but develops a new lesson. They argue that in the parable the first were not really made last nor the last made first. The grumbling of the first workers was because their pay was made *equal* to the pay of the last workers. They did not complain, so the argument goes, that they had been *subordinated*.

None the less, we prefer the opinion that this paradoxical sentence does express a truth directly taught by the parable and is an integral part of it. Jesus, we recall, introduced the parable as a proof of "Many shall be last who are first, and first who are last" (Mt. 19:30). Hence, the paradox at the end merely repeats the lesson presented at the beginning.

Moreover, the parable is at pains to give the men their pay in the inverse order of the amount of their work. The generosity of the owner (God) makes the last men first as to the *rate* of their reward and the *time* of their payment. To this extent it clearly seems to subordinate the first workers.

The entire account is a reminder to all of us that everything we have, whether spiritual or temporal, is the gift of God. If God in His infinite wisdom and love gives more to others, we have no right to complain, inasmuch as God alone has made us all that we are. The pauper given a million dollars cannot justly resent a gift twice as large to another pauper.

THE TWO SONS

Mt. 21:28–32

"A man had two sons; and he went to the first and said, 'Son, go and work today in my vineyard.' 'I will not,' he answered; but afterward he repented and went. Then, going to the second, he made the same request. 'I will, Sir,' he replied, but did not go. Which of the two did the father's will?"

"The first," they told Him. Jesus said to them, "Indeed, I tell you that the publicans and the harlots will go into the Kingdom of God before you. For John came to you on a mission of right-eousness, and you did not believe him; but the publicans and the harlots believed him; while you, though you saw this, did not even afterward repent so as to believe him."

Jesus spoke this parable toward the end of His life, when the opposition of the chief priests and elders was becoming more acrid and vocal. The present story was explained by Jesus Him-self, and therefore should present little or no difficulty.

A man had two sons, whom he requested to work in his vineyard. The first refused to go, then changed his mind and went. The second agreed to work, but actually did not do so.

The comparison reminds us of the frequent biblical allusions to Israel as the vineyard and to God as the owner. By Jesus' own explanation the "vineyard" here is the kingdom of God. The publicans and harlots, sinners as they were, did not listen at first to God's law; they "refused to go." When, however, John the Baptist preached his mission of righteousness to them, they repented of their former stubborn bad will. The Pharisees and Sadducees, on the other hand, professed all along to be doers of God's word, just as the second son in the parable claimed to be obedient. None the less, when they heard John's preaching they remained obstinate in not accepting his message, which was, after all, the message of the owner of the vineyard. Hence, by their own admission in answer to Jesus' query regarding His parable, they did not do the will of God because they equivalently were acting like the second son.

By this parable Jesus also made it even more clear that the mission of John the Baptist had the same purpose as His own, namely, to teach the will of God. At the minimum He thus implicitly claimed for Himself the divine authority of a prophet. His earlier claims that He was the fulfillment of John's preaching meant that He was someone even greater.

THE WICKED TENANTS

Mt. 21:33–45

"Listen to another parable: There was a householder who planted a vineyard, surrounded it with a fence, dug out a wine-vat in it, and erected a watch-tower; then he let it out to vine-dressers, and went abroad. And when the fruit season was at hand, he sent his servants to the vine-dressers to receive his share of the fruit. But the vine-dressers, seizing his servants, beat one, murdered another, and stoned another. He again sent other servants more in number than the former; and they treated them the same way. Afterward he sent his son to them, saying, 'They will reverence my son.' The vine-dressers, however, on seeing the son, said among themselves, 'This is the heir; come let us kill him, and take his inheritance!' Accordingly, they seized him, flung him outside the vineyard, and murdered him. When, therefore, the owner of the vineyard comes, what will he do to these vine-dressers?" They answered Him, "He will miserably destroy those miserable men, and will let out the vineyard to other vine-dressers, who will pay him his share of the fruit at the time it is due."

Jesus said to them, "Have you never read in the Scriptures, 'A stone which the builders rejected—that was made the corner-stone—it was the Lord's doing, and it is marvelous in our eyes'? Therefore, I tell you, the Kingdom of God shall be taken away from you and given to a nation producing its fruits. And he who falls upon this Stone shall be broken in pieces; but upon whomever it will fall, it shall scatter him as dust!"

Mk. 12:1–12

He now began to speak to them in parables: "A man planted a vineyard, surrounded it with a fence, dug out a wine-vat, and erected a watch-tower; then he let it out to vine-dressers, and went abroad. And at the proper season he sent a servant to the vine-dressers, so that he might receive from the vine-dressers his share of the fruit of the vineyard. But seizing the servant, they beat him, and sent him off with nothing. And again he sent another servant to them; but they wounded him in the head, and treated him with indignity. And he sent another, and him they murdered; and so with many others, either beating or murdering them. Having yet one, a dearly loved son, he sent him to them last, saying, 'They will reverence my son.' Those vine-dressers, however, said to one another, 'This is the heir; come, let us kill him, and the inheritance shall be ours!' Accordingly, they seized him, murdered him, and flung him outside the vineyard. What, therefore, will the owner of the vineyard do? He will come and bring destruction upon the vine-dressers, and will give the vineyard to others. Have you not read this passage of Scripture: 'A Stone which the builders rejected—that was made the corner-stone—it was the Lord's doing, and it is marvelous in our eyes'?" And they would fain have arrested Him but for their dread of the populace; for they knew that He had related this parable against them.

Lk. 20:9–19

He also began to relate this parable to the people: "A man planted a vineyard, and let it out to vine-dressers, and went abroad for a long time. And at the proper season he sent a servant to the vine-dressers, so that they might give him his share of the fruit of the vineyard. But the vine-dressers beat him, and sent him off with nothing. And he sent still another servant; but they beat him also, treated him with indignity, and sent him off with nothing. And he sent still a third; and this one they wounded, and flung him out. Then the owner of the vineyard said, 'What shall I do? I will send my beloved son; perhaps they will reverence him.' The vine-dressers, however, on seeing him reasoned among themselves, 'This is the heir; let us kill him, in order that the inheritance may be ours.' Accordingly they flung him outside the vineyard and murdered him. What therefore will the owner of the vineyard do to them? He will come and bring destruction upon these vine-dressers, and will give the vineyard to others." On hearing this, they said, "God forbid!"

But He, fixing on them His gaze, said, "What then means this that is written: 'A Stone which the builders rejected,—that one was made the Corner stone'? Every one who falls upon that stone shall be broken to pieces; but upon whomsoever it shall fall, it shall grind him to dust!" And the scribes and the chief priests wished to lay hands on Him that very moment, yet they dreaded the populace; for they knew that He had told this parable against them.

If one were to seek out a parable of Jesus which would exemplify the theory behind the typical Hebrew parable, the present story of the wicked tenants would qualify among the top contenders. First, there occurs the description of a scene generally true to life, a vineyard rented to tenant farmers or vinedressers, with its fence, wine vat, and watchtower.

Next, the parable sends the owner off to a far country for a vaguely long absence. From this distance the owner dispatches servants to collect the rent from the tenants. The parable, noting that one servant after the other is murdered by the wicked farmers, still wishes to tell its outline of Jewish religious history. Hence, it departs from reality in that the owner fails to take the strong measures ordinarily necessary to stop such plunder and murder. Instead, pacifically enough, he reasons that the wicked men will reverence his own son even though they have killed his hired servants. He sends his son, too. The son, of course, meets the same bad fate. We note that the owner will take vengeance only after he has permitted his tenants to cap their previous crimes with this, the most heinous of all.

Jesus puts the conclusion of the story in the form of a question to His listeners, many of whom are His sworn enemies. This procedure, too, follows the set form of question-answer between the Jewish religious teacher and his pupils. Under Jesus' skillful direction it forces His enemies to reply, "The owner will miserably destroy those miserable men and will let out the vineyard to other vine-dressers, who will pay him his share of the fruit at the time it is due." As Luke reports this, some of the listeners exclaim, "God forbid!"—so well did they recognize the import of the parable and their places in it.

Now Jesus injects direct allegory into the narrative by explaining the parable's meaning in terms of a rejected cornerstone. For modern readers it may be necessary to explain that the reference here is not to the merely decorative "cornerstone" in which mementos of a building's dedication are enclosed. As a unit of the building, such a hollow block is no more important than the most obscure common brick. The stone in question in the parable is an angle stone crowning and uniting two walls, literally at their corner.

Jesus first interprets the detail that it is a stone so that it becomes a stumbling block for whoever falls upon it. Then He changes the emphasis so that the stone will scatter as dust whomever it falls upon. Thus, the parable veers at will throughout its course from general lessons to detailed, exact allegory.

We can have no doubt about the reason for Jesus' choice of the vineyard. The setting of His previous story of the two sons is to be continued here even more vividly. Every devout Jew would know the vineyard of God mentioned in Isaiah (5), and the details given there. Jesus takes over the picture and adds more contemporary descriptions of a vineyard which, however, do not figure in the final lesson but are inserted only for literary color. The servants of the master, who is undoubtedly God, are the prophets whom God sent to Israel and to Juda. The beating, murdering, and stoning which Jesus mentioned were not confined to the imaginary servants of the parable.

But the master stroke of Jesus' reasoning lies in His choice of the owner's son as the last in the series of representatives sent to receive the rent. Here again we see the advantages of the parabolic way of teaching. In a manner veiled in appearance yet unmistakably clear to His enemies Jesus not only claims His unique natural sonship of God, but also prophesies His death. Even the immediate motive for the crucifixion is practically revealed here in the parable: If the new law of Jesus were to take hold, the old, established order would have to be overturned, and those who were profiting from it would lose out.

The parable says still more. The owner will eject the wicked vine dressers and will rent his land to new tenants "who will pay him his share of fruit at the time it is due." This, too, the listening Pharisees understood, as their "God forbid!" indicated.

To repeat the prophecy of this impending substitution, Jesus quotes Psalm 117:22 and 23, "A stone which the builders rejected, that was made the corner-stone, it was the Lord's doing, and it is marvelous in our eyes." Originally, this seems to have been a Jewish proverb referring to the rejection of the Jews by the pagan nations in contrast to the special vocation they had as God's Chosen People.

But now, Jesus says—to resume—"The Kingdom of God shall be taken away from you and given to a nation producing its fruits." Here is still another indication of the supplanting of those who in God's plan were originally to be the first to accept the good tidings of Jesus' law of love. Four times, then, Jesus warns of what is coming, yet all in vain. Even though "the chief priests and Pharisees . . . perceived that He was speaking about them," their only reaction was the desire to arrest Him; they were deterred only by their fear of the populace. Yet their very rejection of His message was true to His prophecy of the rejection of the cornerstone, which in this case was Jesus Himself.

THE GREAT BANQUET

Lk. 14:15–24

One of His fellow-guests . . . said to Him, "Happy is he who shall feast in the Kingdom of God!" He replied to him, "A man gave a grand banquet, and invited many people; and he sent his servant at the time of the banquet to tell those who had been invited to come, for all was now ready. But they all with one accord began to excuse themselves. The first told him, 'I have bought some land, and am obliged to go out and see it; I beg thee have me excused.' Another said, 'I have bought five yoke of oxen, and am going to try them; I beg thee have me excused.' And another said, 'I have married a wife, and owing to this I am unable to come.' The servant accordingly came and reported all this to his master. Then the master of the house was angry, and said to the servant, 'Go out right away into the streets and alleys of the city, and bring in here the poor and the maimed and the blind and the lame!' The servant reported, 'What you have ordered, sir, has been done, and there is yet room.' Then the master said to the servant, 'Go out into the roads and along the hedges, and compel people to come in, so that my house may be filled! For I tell you, that not one of those men that were invited shall taste of my banquet!' "

In the order of parables which we are following, Matthew places at this point the parable of the wedding feast and the guest without nuptial garment (22:1–14). A difficulty thereby occurs whether the story of the wedding feast as given in Matthew is the same as that of the great banquet given in Luke. The consideration of the parable in Luke will not only highlight its own lesson but will also suggest the reasons for deciding whether Jesus proposed *two* parables with a similar setting or whether *one* appears with different meanings and different emphasis in the two evangelists.

Our habits of modern etiquette vary somewhat from the technique of invitation implied in Luke. The man giving his banquet has already invited his guests, who evidently have accepted his offer. Now at the time when the banquet is prepared, he sends his servant merely to remind them that their banquet is ready. If we understand this existence of a previously accepted invitation, we can realize the full discourtesy of rudely refusing the servant's notice.

The excuses in the parable are evidently not intended to be used as part of the lesson, although in an applied sense they could become an occasion to draw a moral. At any rate, the first man's excuse concerns his need to inspect a plot of land before he closes the final sale. The second man is less polite. Real necessity does not exist for his immediate testing of the five yoke of oxen he has just purchased, but he alleges the fact as his reason. The third man is the rudest of all. Asking no pardon, he merely says that he is unable to come, for he has "married a wife." That does not seem to imply, as some have claimed, that his wedding feast is now being celebrated; he merely wishes to stay at home with his new bride.

On the lighter side this comment of the parable has been jokingly used in our day to exemplify the pressures of family life. Whereas the other men felt constrained to excuse themselves, the husband is pictured as stating that the fact of his domestic alliance is enough to do away with all his former liberty in going where he will—and anyone should be aware of it without further ado!

But the parable is serious, and the master of the house becomes angry when his servant brings him the reports. He dispatches the servants again, not once but twice—a vivid literary device to emphasize the need for filling the house, and the size of the banquet. Those to come now are the poor, the maimed, the blind, the lame, and those of the roads and hedges who have no shelter. The conclusion of the master is that "not one of those men that were invited shall taste of my banquet!"

Jesus must have frequently used this comparison of the kingdom of God as a great banquet. Here the lesson is that the original invitation to the learned Pharisees and scribes to accept Christ's new law was rejected. The invitation, then, will go to the common folk whom the leaders despise, and these folk will receive Jesus as their Messiah.

Over and above this lesson, it does not seem that the parable should be pressed further, as if some deeper meaning were to exist in the excuses given by the three men, or in the identity of the servant, or in the various classes of poor folk admitted later. For ourselves, however, we can discern a lesson in the parable which can well apply to our private lives. When the invitation of God comes to us to do His will in any way, we are not justified in alleging flimsy pretexts to evade what is evidently our duty.

*　　*　　*

Great scripture scholars are ranged on both sides of the question whether this parable is actually the same as the wedding feast reported by Matthew. We suggest here the opinion that it stands by itself.

a. As for the common theme of a banquet, this in itself would not argue to identity, precisely because a banquet was so logical to use as a setting for the kingdom of God. Jesus would also be logical in using the comparison more than once.

b. This banquet in Luke, moreover, is merely a supper given by an unnamed man. In Matthew it is a wedding feast given by a king for his son.

c. In Luke no violence is done to the single servant reminding the future guests. In Matthew the many servants given this task are maltreated and murdered.

d. The lesson in Luke seems to be restricted to extending the message of the kingdom to the ordinary Jews after the message had been rejected by their leaders. In Matthew the lesson strongly emphasizes the rejection of Israel by God because the nation did not accept Jesus as its Messiah. The supplanting of the Jews by the gentiles is also implied.

e. Matthew adds to his main narrative a second and completely independent unit, the guest without the wedding garment. This is a reminder that the gentiles, too, must be fit to attend the wedding feast. There does not seem to be room for this development in Luke.

f. We admit that Matthew's gospel usually presents the discourses of Jesus within a topical rather than chronological framework. Hence, the time when the parable of the wedding feast was uttered cannot be determined too precisely. None the less, since it logically fits with the other parables in Matthew appearing in the closing days of Jesus' life, the story of the wedding feast was apparently given much later than the parable of the great banquet, which Luke presents as occurring several months before the death of Jesus.

THE WEDDING BANQUET

Mt. 22:1–10

"The Kingdom of Heaven may be compared to a king, who made a wedding banquet for his son. And he sent his servants to notify those who had been invited to the wedding; but they would not come. He again sent other servants, saying, 'Tell the invited, Behold, I have prepared my banquet, my bullocks and fat calves are killed, and everything is ready; come to the wedding.' But they made light of it, and went off, one to his farm, another to his traffic; while the rest, seizing his servants, maltreated and murdered them. But the king on learning this was enraged, and sending his troops he destroyed those murderers, and burned their city. Then he said to his servants, 'The wedding is ready, but those invited were unworthy. Go, then, into the thoroughfares, and invite to the wedding-banquet as many as you find.' Those servants accordingly went into the streets and collected all whom they found, both bad and good; and the wedding-hall was filled with guests."

Once again Jesus compares the kingdom of Heaven to a banquet. A king sends his servants to notify those previously invited that the wedding feast of his son is ready. Two types of reactions occur. One group of would-be guests is completely indifferent to the reminder, going off to their farms and to their business. The others maltreat and murder the king's servants. Enraged, the king sends his troops to destroy the murderers and burn their city. A second time he dispatches the servants, this time to bring in all they can find to fill the hall for the wedding feast.

At this point we set the actual limit of the parable, for the ensuing description of the guest without the wedding garment seems to be a second parable fused with the story of the banquet (as we shall immediately explain in the next pages). The parable is particularly ominous in mentioning the burning of the murderers' city. Some commentators have seen in this a literal prophecy of the future fall of Jerusalem and its sack by the Romans. We prefer a more conservative opinion; namely, that Jesus is merely continuing a vivid literary description of how the power of the great king cannot be mocked. Otherwise, the avenging king would be made a pagan Roman emperor, and this certainly cannot stand with the clear symbolism of the parable that the king is God.

Following as it does the parables of the two sons, the wicked tenants, and the cornerstone, the meaning of this parable is little in doubt. As we said, God has the role of the king, and Jesus the Messiah is the son. The servants are the prophets, whose message was received by Israel sometimes with contempt, sometimes with indifference, sometimes with hostility ending in murder. But God is not mocked, and in His own time He brings destruction on those who hinder the spread of the kingdom. Those who willfully reject and obstruct the kingdom of God on earth will themselves be violently rejected and punished for their sinful obstinacy.

The second group of servants, succeeding the murdered prophets, are the apostles of Jesus, who will now take the message of salvation to the gentiles because it has been refused by those for whom it was first destined. It is noteworthy that with the latitude of meaning typical of the parable, the guests of the streets are both good and bad. Here we see a recurrence of the theme first proposed in the parables of the darnel weed and the fish net; namely, even among those who enter the kingdom of Heaven on earth there will be found bad mixed with good.

The rejection of the Jews as the first recipients of Christ's teaching is certainly the capital lesson of the parable. We should emphasize, however, that this refers to the *official* rejection by the nation *as a whole;* the fact exists that practically all the first Christians were converted from Judaism. Even when the apostles did their preaching, they went first to the synagogues and only later to the gentiles after they had been expelled. The Acts of the Apostles gives us a sample of this attitude in Peter's conduct, particularly his surprise that the Holy Spirit came upon the gentiles as well as the converted Jews (Acts 10:35, 45). Paul (in Acts 13:46) also went first to the Jews and only later to the gentiles. These actions of the apostles are our best indication how they themselves understood the words of Jesus in parables like this.

THE GUEST WITHOUT A
WEDDING GARMENT

Mt. 22:11–14

"Now the king came in to look at the guests; and he observed there a man who was not wearing a wedding-robe; and he said to him, 'My good friend, how didst thou get in here without a wedding-robe?' He, however, was speechless. Then the king said to the attendants, 'Tie him hand and foot, and fling him into the darkness outside; there shall be the weeping and the grinding of teeth.' For many are called, but few are chosen."

There is good reason to hold that Matthew's passage of the guest without the wedding garment is a fragment of a parable, and was fused with the story of the wedding feast. By whom was this done? One theory proposes that Matthew combined the parable of the feast with another banquet parable in which the wedding-garment motif was prominent; he used the one not only in its independent right but also as an introduction to the other, since their settings were the same. Nor would he have acted contrary to accepted ancient canons of history in editing and adjusting his material in this fashion, provided he faithfully retained the substantial truth.

It seems more likely, however, that Jesus Himself was responsible for the combination. Earlier we mentioned how He presented the kingdom under the literary figure of a banquet. In this He built upon Jewish tradition concerning the messianic banquet when the anointed of the Lord would come in the glory of the kingdom. The parable as Jesus used it was a literary vehicle capable of all sorts of adaptations in order to teach various lessons. Accordingly, He could easily have first presented the wedding feast to teach the rejection of the Jewish nation, its supplanting by the gentiles, and the presence of good and bad after the gentiles entered the kingdom. A kind of literary economy on His part would then employ the already established setting to inculcate the need for the proper dispositions in belonging to the kingdom. Thus, the story of the guest who lacked conventional garb would be more than a mere appendix and would teach its lesson on its own.

Ancient etiquette is said to be reflected in the parable in so far as the king "came in to look at the guests." According to the dignity of his position the king would not himself eat with the diners at the banquet. He would, however, condescend to walk through the friendly gathering.

In the parable he notes the serious breach of good manners, the veritable insult on the part of a guest wearing ordinary clothes and not the ceremonial robe that should have been donned on such an occasion. The king addresses him quite gently, "My good friend, how did you get in here without a wedding robe?" Twentieth century readers belonging to an occidental culture have thought that the guest was condemned with his case unheard. The speechlessness of the man does not have this meaning. If any good reason existed, it should have been voiced at this time, or at least there should have been an equivalent apology.

In an attempt to relieve the appearance of ruthless injustice done to the man, some ancient writers made the supposition that the host on such an occasion would provide proper robes for his guests, and this man failed to make use of the service. Very little evidence exists to substantiate any such custom, and the gospel account gives no hint of it here. Other writers have conjectured that in the rush of being invited without advance notice there was no time to become properly vested. Even this can hardly be sustained.

The point of the parable is that a gross insult was done to the king. That is always the lesson, taking it for granted that the insult was deliberate, grave, and without mitigating circumstances. Hence, the punishment is equally severe. Bound hand and foot, the erstwhile guest is flung outside the lighted banquet chamber into the darkness outside. Jesus' words now move from the figurative language of the parable and merge into its lesson.

The darkness outside the banquet is fused with the "exterior darkness" which occurs in Matthew to designate the place of the damned (Mt. 8:12; 25:30). Thus, the eternal condemnation for deliberate unforgiven sin is here exemplified. It is further indicated by the "weeping and the grinding of teeth"—the impotent rage of the damned—which we met in Matthew (13:42), where the useless darnel weed is thrown into the fire and burned.

"Many are called, but few are chosen."

Because of the many possibilities for misunderstanding the parable's final phrase, "Many are called, but few are chosen," we should first determine what it certainly does *not* mean. We are safe in excluding it as a direct reference made by Jesus to indicate the number of the damned or the number of the saved.

Yet even here not every argument leading to this conclusion proves its point. For instance, one might think that the possible reference to eternal salvation is out of the question because Jesus says, "*Many* are called," instead of the correct fact that *all* are called to salvation by God. This argument does not hold true. The reason is that the Greek word for "many" is often used in the New Testament with the meaning of "all." Thus in Mark 10:45 we read, "The Son of Man . . . came . . . to give His life a ransom for many"—certainly for all. At the Last Supper Jesus said, "This is My Blood of the Covenant, which is poured out for many"—again for all (Mk. 14:24). Therefore, we must logically understand the phrase as "All the multitude are called, but few are chosen."

Jesus was repeatedly asked by His listeners about the number of the saved, but He never gave a direct answer. When "some one asked Him, 'Lord, are they few who are saved?' . . . He said to them: 'Strive to enter by the narrow door; for many, I tell you, will seek to enter it, and shall be unable'" (Lk. 13:24). In other words the entrance is narrow in the sense Jesus means: self-renunciation is necessary. One's entrance depends upon one's will to accomplish it.

Jesus' evasiveness on this subject is all the more remarkable in view of the prevalent tradition in Jewish literature of His time that very few would be saved. It would have been very easy for

Him to go along with the popular belief, but Jesus refused either to agree or to disagree with it. Instead, he reiterated the need for personal effort to save one's soul. There was no need to satisfy a curiosity with speculative knowledge that would be of no profit to one's own salvation. By His teaching on eternal punishment and His reference to the broad way to destruction (Mt. 7:13-14), He revealed the fact of damnation for some; but, we repeat, Jesus was equally adamant in refusing to teach more than this. The subject was a mystery to be concealed in the infinite wisdom of God.

Moreover, "few" and "many" are terms so relative that one cannot deduce from Jesus' words whether or not the greater part of mankind is saved or lost. When we consider His position soberly, the stand He adopted appears as the only reasonable one to take. He told His listeners in so many words that *their salvation depended on themselves*, though in cooperation with God's grace. The apostles taught the same tradition from Him, that no one is excluded "in the sight of God our Saviour, who wishes all men to be saved" (1 Tim. 2:4). For all these reasons, then, we cannot see how Jesus would explain in "many are called but few are chosen" a truth which elsewhere He consistently refused to divulge.

None the less, if some one were still to insist on an interpretation of this phrase as a rigid prophecy of damnation, reasoning that is equally specious could be used to prove the exact opposite. Of all the members at the banquet, only one was without a wedding garment and was ejected; would not a like minority of mankind be ejected into eternal darkness? But the answer is, of course, that the parable teaches nothing on the subject of damnation; and also that the guest might represent a class instead of an individual—therefore indicating a great multitude. In any event the example is useful to show how diametrically opposite meanings can be obtained by juggling scripture texts without regard for the body of revealed Christian teaching.

All this, however, does not reach the root of what the "many are called" phrase really means. It evidently refers neither to the wedding feast nor to the wedding-garment episode, but is a general truth summing up the gist of both parables. *It teaches in a very strong way that all members of the human race are called by God. Those who are not chosen are rejected because of their bad will.* The "few chosen" phrase becomes a strong paradox to the "many." Not all of the "many" follow their lights to enter the kingdom, whether they be among the Jews first invited or among the gentiles who supplant them in the kingdom of Christ.

Since all rejection from the kingdom is ultimately because of the individual's bad will, we have no fear for the souls who are the "other sheep" (to change the metaphor momentarily), namely, those who have not yet entered Christ's kingdom through no fault of their own. By some means or other Jesus can bring them to His kingdom and to His banquet clothed in the wedding garment of their love of God.

THE NARROW DOOR

Lk. 13:22-30

Some one asked Him, "Lord, are they few who are saved?" But He said to them: "Strive to enter by the narrow door; for many, I tell you, will seek to enter it, and shall be unable. When once the master of the house has risen and closed the door, and you begin, standing outside, to knock at the door, saying, 'Lord, open to us!' and he shall say to you in answer, 'I know not whence you are!'—then you will begin to say, 'It is we who ate and drank in Thy company and Thou didst teach in our streets'; and he will say, 'I tell you, I know not whence you are! Begone from me, all you doers of iniquity.' There shall be the weeping and the grinding of teeth, when you see Abraham, Isaac and Jacob, and all the prophets in the Kingdom of God, and you yourselves thrust out. And they shall come from east and west, and from north and south, and shall recline in the Kingdom of God. And behold, some are last who shall be first, and some are first who shall be last."

This parable resembles the words of Jesus in Matthew (7:13–14) concerning the narrow door to salvation. It differs, however, in that it applies primarily to Jewish acceptance of Jesus' kingdom instead of referring to salvation for all. The stage is set for it with the explicit question of a disciple, "Lord, are they few who are saved?"—a question that reflects, as we mentioned, the then current notion that the saved would be relatively few.

Strikingly, Jesus does not give the question a direct answer. That in itself is indication enough that we are in the presence of a mystery whose solution is known to God alone. Moreover, since Jesus did not reveal it to us, such knowledge is evidently neither necessary nor even useful for our individual salvation. Nor can we make any conclusion about salvation from Jesus' words, "Strive to enter by the narrow door." This merely means, again to repeat, that the way to save one's soul requires self-renunciation as a necessary means to the end.

As the parable begins to develop, its application to the Jewish nation becomes more evident. The narrow door which requires effort on the part of him who enters becomes the door of the house which is shut by the master against those who are knocking, much as we read in the parable of the ten virgins. These people outside identify themselves as having eaten and drunk in the master's company, and they remind him that he taught in their streets. Thus, the allusion to Jesus' contemporaries is all too clear.

But the master is inflexible by now. He quotes Psalm 6:9, "Begone from me, all you doers of iniquity," following with a further quotation from Isaiah (49:12; 59:19) that the gentiles from the four corners of the earth will "recline in the Kingdom of God." This is a reference to the eternal banquet of the Messiah, phrased according to the custom of reclining on the banquet couches. Here, too, in the kingdom with the gentiles will be Abraham, Isaac, and Jacob, as well as all the prophets—but "you yourselves will be thrust out." It is indeed a dire prediction that the Jews will be rejected from the Church of Christ unless they change their obstinacy in refusing Him as their anointed saviour.

Understanding the parable in this light, any possible misunderstanding of it in a sense of unjust reprobation of part of mankind is precluded. Because the question is so momentous, we wish to summarize for a last time the reasons for these judgments:

1. Jesus refuses to answer the question as to the number saved.

2. The narrow door of which Jesus speaks symbolizes the effort required to be saved. If it represented a relatively low number of the saved, it would be an answer which Jesus steadfastly is unwilling to give.

3. The shutting of the narrow door against those who knock cannot and does not mean that some souls are locked out of Heaven despite their earnest pleas to enter. In the parable they are locked out of Christ's kingdom on earth, His Church, not because He turns them away but because they have previously refused to accept His preaching when He revealed His doctrine to them.

4. The mention of "some are last who shall be first, and some are first who shall be last," describes the gentiles' acceptance of Christ (and therefore their preference in that respect) in the face of Jewish rejection of Jesus (and therefore an equivalent loss of preference).

THE TEN VIRGINS

Mt. 25:1–13

"Then the Kingdom of Heaven shall be compared to ten virgins, who, taking their lamps, went out to meet the bridegroom. And five of them were foolish, and five were wise; for the foolish, though they brought their lamps, took no oil with them; but the wise took oil in their flasks along with the lamps. While, however, the bridegroom delayed, they all slumbered and slept. But at midnight a cry was raised, 'Lo, the bridegroom! Come forth to meet him!' Then all those virgins rose, and trimmed their lamps. And the foolish said to the wise ones, 'Give us some of your oil, for our lamps are going out.' But the wise ones replied, 'For fear there should not be enough for us and for you, you had better go to the shopkeepers, and buy some for yourselves.' While, however, they went to buy, the bridegroom came; and those who were ready went in with him to the wedding-feast; and the door was closed. Afterward came the other virgins also, crying, 'Lord, Lord, open to us!' But his answer was, 'Indeed, I tell you, I know you not!' Watch, therefore, because you know not the day nor the hour."

The details of this parable afford an occasion to summarize the marriage customs of Jesus' time even though (according to parabolic license) some parts of the story do not agree with everyday experience. The "ten virgins" are bridesmaids in modern parlance. "Ten" in itself has no particular significance. It was evidently chosen as a round number. Nor does the term "virgin" have any special significance here with regard to virginity. The word is used in the sense of "maiden" or "young girl." When preachers or ancient writers have drawn lessons concerning virginity, such explanations are an application that goes beyond the parable's meaning as such.

In thinking of the marriage customs in Jesus' time we must rid our minds of preconceived set notions gleaned from modern experience. The Jewish marriage then consisted essentially of two parts, what we might call the "espousal" and the "wedding." The espousal, however, was not the engagement, the promise of future marriage which it is today. It represented a valid though incomplete marriage, and the espoused groom and bride were considered husband and wife even though they did not live together. The interval of living apart for a year had evidently been introduced because of an economic consideration, namely, the need to prepare a suitable home.

We are not absolutely certain of the obligations of the espousal with regard to conception and birth of a child. Although somewhat varying testimonies exist, it seems that a child conceived or born within the year of espousal would be considered legitimate, provided that the espoused husband accepted the child as his own. (Jesus was miraculously conceived in Mary's womb within this year of espousal. The gospel phrase "Joseph took her unto himself" or "received his wife" (Mt. 1:24) is generally interpreted as a reference to the second ceremony of marriage, when Joseph took Mary to live in his own home.)

The wedding in the parable of the ten virgins is, then, the second ceremony, that is, the solemnization of the marriage with external pomp, and the time when the bride waited to receive the groom, to be brought to his house. The happy couple were escorted by male friends of the groom (translated sometimes as "children of the bridegroom"—cf. Mt. 9:15) and female friends of the bride, such as the present ten virgins. These wedding celebrations would begin in the late afternoon and evening and might last the whole night through, if not for several days.

For the purposes of the parable's lesson, the bridesmaids hold only small terra cotta lamps, which soon exhaust their oil supply as the wedding party awaits the groom. If they had had torches, which were also customary, the situation of the parable could hardly have occurred. On several other counts, too, Jesus tailored His story to fit the lesson He desired. Thus, when the five foolish virgins find they have no more oil for their lamps, they are told to go to the shopkeepers to buy more, and forthwith leave on their errand. The fact is that shops would hardly be open at the middle of the night, as represented in the parable.

Then suddenly the narrative moves into its lesson while not completely deserting the story of the wedding. The doors of the groom's house are locked against the foolish virgins when they return with their oil, and this is hardly a feature of a true wedding. They address the groom, "Lord, Lord, open to us!"—and he replies in all earnestness that he knows them not. No longer is he the earthly master and groom, for his title suggests the eternal Lord, Jesus Himself. Jesus thus is already teaching that if we are not ready with a record of virtue when God calls us, God will equivalently tell us that He "knows us not."

It is interesting that in the best manuscript readings the parable mentions a watch only for the groom. The bride as such is given no notice. In this we see Jesus' thought continuing the frequent Old Testament theme that God is the spouse of Israel His bride, and that the golden age of the Messiah is represented by a wedding feast. For a listener steeped in Jewish literature, the implicit meaning of Jesus could hardly be missed.

Sometimes lessons are drawn from this parable according to the sentence, "When the bridegroom delayed in coming, they all became drowsy and slept." The parable is evidently not thinking of the sleep of spiritual sloth, for, after all, even the prudent no less than the foolish virgins slept! This prudence, moreover, of the virgins who brought extra oil with them is a very worldly sort of wisdom. Their conduct is anything but charitable when they refuse to share their stores with the rest, and send them off to purchase oil on their own.

The true lesson is evidently a warning to be ready for God's call. Jesus makes this explicit with His closing comment, "Watch, therefore, because you know not the day nor the hour." Since the parable follows the eschatological discourse in which Jesus spoke of His judgment at the end of the world, and since it occurs in context with other exhortations to watchfulness, its direct reference seems to be the unexpected suddenness of Christ's second coming. For our personal lives we can draw a further lesson, in making the logical application to the suddenness of death. We should always be prepared for God's call to judgment when our time comes to die.

THE TALENTS—THE GOLD PIECES

Mt. 25:14–30

"For it is as when a man on going abroad called his servants, and intrusted them with his property. And to one he gave five talents, to another two, and to another one—to each in proportion to his ability—and took his departure. Then the one who had received the five talents went at once and traded with them, and made five more. And likewise he who had received the two made two more. But he who had received the one went off and dug a hole in the ground, and hid his lord's money.

"Now, after a long time the master of those servants returned, and settled accounts with them. And the one who had received the five talents came bringing five talents more, saying, 'My lord, thou didst intrust me with five talents; see, I have made five talents more!' His lord said to him, 'Well done, good and faithful servant! Thou hast been faithful over a little, I will set thee over much. Enter into the joy of thy lord!' Then he also who had received two talents came and said, 'My lord, thou didst intrust me with two talents; see, I have made two talents more!' His master said to him, 'Well done, good and faithful servant! Thou hast been faithful over a little, I will set thee over much. Enter into the joy of thy lord!' And he also who had received the one talent came and said, 'My lord, I knew thee to be a hard man; thou reapest where thou hast not sown, and gatherest where thou hast not scattered; and being afraid, I went and hid thy talent in the ground. See—thou hast what is thine!' But his master said in reply, 'Thou wicked and indolent slave! Thou wast aware that I reap where I have not sown, and gather where I have not scattered: thou oughtest, for that reason, to have invested my money with the bankers; then, on my return, I should have received my own with the interest. Take, therefore, that talent away from him, and give it to him who has the ten talents. For to every one who possesses, more shall be given, and he shall have abundance; but from him who possesses not, even that which he has shall be taken away. And cast that useless slave into the outer darkness; there shall be the weeping and the grinding of teeth!' "

Lk. 19:12–27

"A nobleman . . . traveled to a distant country to receive a kingdom for himself, and to return. And calling ten of his servants, he gave them ten gold-pieces, and said to them, 'Trade with these until I come.' Now his countrymen hated him; so they sent an embassy after him with the petition, 'We are not willing that this person should reign over us.' On his return, after having obtained the kingdom, he ordered those servants to whom he had given the money to be summoned, in order that he might ascertain how much each one had made in his business transactions. So the first appeared, saying, 'My lord, thy gold-piece has made ten gold-pieces more.' 'Well done, good servant!' he said to him, 'because thou hast been faithful with a very little, thou shalt have the government of ten cities.' Then the second came, saying, 'My lord, thy gold-piece has made five gold-pieces.' And to him also he said, 'And thou shalt be governor of five cities.' Another also came, saying, 'Here, my lord, is thy gold-piece, which I have laid away in a napkin; for I was afraid of thee, because thou art a hard man; thou takest up what thou didst not deposit, and thou reapest what thou didst not sow.' He said to him, 'Out of thine own mouth will I condemn thee, thou wicked slave. Thou knewest me to be a hard man, taking up what I did not deposit, and reaping what I did not sow. Why, then, didst thou not put my money in the bank, so that on my return I could have exacted it with the interest. Take the gold-piece from him,' he said to the attendants, 'and give it to the one who has the ten gold-pieces.' 'Lord,' they said to him, 'he has ten gold-pieces!' So, I tell you, that to every one who possesses shall be given; but from him who possesses not, even what he has shall be taken away from him. But as for those enemies of mine who did not wish me to reign over them, bring them here, and execute them in my presence.''

These are two separate parables, but their lesson is identical: God's gifts, whether natural or supernatural, should be used properly. As would be expected, the many similarities in the two narratives suggest the possibility that there was originally one story which later appeared with varying details. We must remember in evaluating this theory that the gospel writers were men of their age, who followed the literary canons of their age. In their acceptance of the primitive Christian traditions about Jesus, the evangelists would have been completely truthful in editing and adjusting their material in order to meet the needs of their audiences. Hence, such a process could have occurred in the present instance with no reflection on the integrity of the authors. None the less, the differences are so marked and the occasions on which the parables were uttered are evidently so far removed that we conclude that Jesus used the same literary framework twice to teach the same lesson.

In Matthew's account a man who goes abroad entrusts his property to three servants, to the amount of ten talents, five, and one, each receiving a sum in proportion to his ability. (The talent in question was a sum of money worth at least $1,200.) It is understood that the servants are to trade with their master's money and return a profit. In the case of the men who received the five and the two talents, their sum is doubled by the time the master returns, and they are given a major reward for having been faithful in a lesser responsibility.

But the man who received the single talent has unprofitably hidden the talent in the ground and so receives a condemnation as a wicked and lazy slave. His single talent is given to the man who already has the ten. Jesus here quotes a paradoxical proverb, "For to every one who possesses, more shall be given, and he shall have abundance; but from him who possesses not, even that which he has shall be taken away." This is but another way of emphasizing the genuine largesse of the master, who does not keep the single unused talent for himself but adds it to the ten won by the energetic servant.

Why should the third man be called wicked and lazy? In one respect he merely tries to manufacture an alibi for his laziness in not trading with the money. The pretext he resorts to only makes his case look worse, for he gives an insolent caricature of his master. "I knew thee to be a hard man, for thou reapest where thou hast not sown, and gatherest where thou hast not scattered." The master, however, refutes him out of his own mouth, revealing the servant's inconsistency. If the money really belonged to a penny-pinching miser, the wicked servant had all the more reason to make a profit from it instead of flinching from his duty and trying to justify his cowardice by an unfair reflection on his master's generosity.

The useless slave is therefore cast into outer darkness (the darkness outside the lights and warmth of the house) where the weeping and the grinding of teeth will occur. Again, Jesus uses certain phrases here which leave the realm of the story and merge into the description of its lesson, eternal punishment. This punishment for those who fail to use God's gifts is signified by darkness and the raging of those who by their bad will have turned away from the eternal Master. Such is the literary device Jesus uses of fusing His narrative with its lesson, just as He has already done when, earlier in the parable, the good servants are told to enter the joy of their lord.

In the parable told by Luke, another thread appears in the story. This is the reference to a nobleman receiving a kingdom. It was apparently prompted by the fact that some of Jesus' listeners supposed that the kingdom of God would make its appearance at once. Jesus tells them accordingly of a nobleman who travels to a distant country to receive a kingdom for himself.

This is a manifest allusion to the custom of princes of the Herodian dynasty to travel to Rome to receive their kingdom from the hands of the emperor. The allusion is equally clear when a few verses later Jesus mentions that the nobleman's "countrymen hated him, so they sent an embassy after him with the petition, 'We are not willing that this person should reign over us.' " Such was the embassy sent to Rome by the Jews in a fruitless attempt to prevent Archelaus from succeeding his father Herod in 4 B.C.

To follow up for ourselves this particular motif to the end, Jesus concludes the parable in the nobleman's words, "As for those enemies of mine who did not wish me to reign over them, bring them here, and execute them in my presence." Jesus is certainly not comparing His kingdom to the petty states of the tyrannical Herodian family, nor could He even suggest a parallel between His ineffable holiness and the bestiality of men like Herod the Great, Archelaus, or Herod Antipas. The heart of the comparison simply points out that His kingdom will not come at once, and until Christ the king returns in the glory of His kingdom, His servants should use profitably the gifts which God gave them. When He does come, He will crush the enemies whose machinations He tolerated to exist before His arrival.

Such, then, is the context within which Luke's parable of the gold pieces fits. The nobleman calls ten servants and gives each of them one gold piece, a *mna* worth some twenty dollars. In only three of these cases do we hear what happens. The first man traffics profitably, making a tenfold profit. He is given charge of ten cities as a reward. The second increases his gold piece fivefold, and he receives five cities.

The third, speaking like the unprofitable servant in Matthew, implicitly reproaches his master for miserliness by means of the excuse of hiding the gold piece in a napkin. This time, however, the only punishment for the wicked slave is the loss of his money, which goes to the man already admired for possessing his ten gold pieces. The paradoxical proverb occurs again, emphasizing as it did in Matthew the generosity of the master, who heaps rewards on those who have been faithful to his commands.

JESUS THE VINE

Jn. 15:1–11

"I am the true vine, and My Father is the vine-dresser. Every branch on Me that does not bear fruit He removes; and every branch that bears fruit He prunes, in order that it may bear more fruit. As for you, you are already pruned, because of the Word I have spoken to you. Abide in Me, and I will abide in you. As the branch cannot bear fruit of itself unless it remains on the vine, so neither can you, unless you remain in Me. I am the vine; you are the branches. He who abides in Me, and I in him, he it is who bears much fruit; because apart from Me you can produce nothing. Whoever does not remain in Me is lopped off like the branch, and withers; and they gather them up and throw them on the fire, and they burn up. If you abide in Me, and My words abide in you, ask for whatever you will, and it shall be done for you. My Father is glorified in this—that you bear plenty of fruit, and so be My disciples. As the Father has loved Me, so have I loved you; continue in my love. If you observe my commandments you shall abide in My love; just as I have observed My Father's commandment, and abide in His love. I have spoken thus to you, in order that my joy may be in you, and your joy may be complete.

"This is my commandment, that you love one another as I have loved you. Greater love has no one than this—that one should lay down one's life for one's friends. You are My friends, if you do what I command you. I no longer call you servants, for the servant is ignorant of what his master does; but I have called you friends, because everything that I heard from My father I have made known to you."

Here is a case in which the lesson fits so many of the parable's details that is has been more often called an allegory than a parable. There is little difficulty in understanding it since Jesus Himself explains the comparisons.

Jesus is the vine, God His Father is the vinedresser. God the Father, working through Jesus, cuts off branches of Jesus that are sterile and dead; but those that bear fruit are pruned in order that they might be even more fruitful. This can be a reminder to us that God deliberately permits and even sends suffering and difficulties into the lives of the good so as to help them reach an even greater supernatural goal.

"As the branch cannot bear fruit of itself unless it remains on the vine, so neither can you, unless you remain in Me. I am the vine; you are the branches. He who abides in Me, and I in him, he it is who bears much fruit; because apart from Me you can produce nothing." This connection with Christ means that in the supernatural order we are completely useless and dead unless we are joined to Jesus by means of sanctifying grace.

A further phrase implies the lessons mentioned elsewhere in this book concerning answered prayer. "If you abide in Me and My words abide in you, ask for whatever you will, and it shall be done for you." Such petitioning must be understood as a request in the proper manner for things that are genuinely good for us in the temporal order and subordinated to the preeminent good in the supernatural order. As usual, Jesus does not promise "when" our prayers will be granted. He does promise that they will infallibly be heard. This is the one logical result of the mutual love existing between the Father and Jesus and His branches, the disciples.

"PHYSICIAN, CURE THYSELF"

Lk. 4:23

He then said to them, "You will doubtless repeat to Me this proverb, 'Physician, cure Thyself!' 'Whatever we have heard has been done at Capharnaum, do also here in Thine own country.' "

There exists a large group of sayings of Jesus which in themselves do not constitute parables in the usual sense of the word, but which none the less impart their teaching by way of a verbal comparison. In numerous instances it is possible that they were first delivered by Jesus in longer form and later compressed into summaries by the evangelists.

Jesus had read a section of the prophet Isaiah in the synagogue at Nazareth, and had applied its meaning to Himself as the Messiah. His fellow Nazarenes, however, wondered at the lowliness of His origin, remarking, "Is not this Joseph's son"—the son of the carpenter? Jesus then quoted the proverb "Physician, cure thyself," not as a parable of His own but as one His countrymen were implicitly uttering. They had demanded miracles of Him here at Nazareth such as they had heard He had done at Capharnaum. He, of course, retorted with still another proverb, that no prophet is acceptable in his own country. This was another way of saying that familiarity breeds contempt, and that local churlish pride prevented the Nazarenes from having the humble faith required if God is to work miracles.

The actual meaning, then, was equivalent to saying, "Since you have been working miracles elsewhere, work them here for your own people. If you cannot do that, you are like a physician curing others but unable to cure himself and members of his own family."

THE SALT

Mt. 5:13

"You are the salt of the earth; but if the salt becomes insipid, with what shall it be salted? It is no longer good for anything but to be thrown out, and trodden under foot by men."

Mk. 9:49–50

"For every one shall be salted with fire. Salt is an excellent thing; but if the salt loses its saltiness, with what will you season it? Have salt in yourselves, and have peace with one another."

Lk. 14:34–35

"Salt is an excellent thing; but if even the salt becomes insipid, what shall it be seasoned with? It is fit neither for the soil nor for the manure-heap; they throw it away."

When Jesus told the disciples that they were the salt of the earth, He did not mean that they were precious as salt, as has sometimes been claimed. Salt was common enough. One can hardly assert that it had special value on the score of being either rare or expensive.

Instead, Jesus reminded the disciples that they had the duty of spreading the preservative influence of Christian doctrine. Just as salt preserves food from corruption, so were they to preserve the world from corrupt doctrine.

The "salt that becomes insipid" was a gospel reference to the results of the many impurities in Palestinian salt obtained from evaporating water of the Dead Sea. These impurities made it easily deliquescent, a viscous mass that was considered useless.

Mark adds Jesus' words that His followers should "have peace with each other" because of having "salt among themselves." This imagery of salt to symbolize friendship was based on the seasoning properties of salt, especially at a common meal of good fellowship.

THE LAMP ON THE LAMPSTAND: THE CITY ON THE MOUNTAIN

Mt. 5:14–15

"You are the light of the world. A city set on a hill cannot be hid. Nor do men light a lamp and place it under the corn-measure, but upon the lampstand; and it gives light to all that are in the house."

Mk. 4:21

"Is the lamp brought in to be placed under the corn-measure or under the bed? Is it not in order to be set upon the lampstand?"

"No one, having lighted a lamp, covers it with a vessel, or puts it under a bed, but places it upon a lampstand, so that those who enter may see the light." "No one having lit a lamp places it in a cellar, or under the corn-measure, but upon the lampstand, so that those who enter may see the light."

Jesus' admonition to be as the lamp on the lampstand is but another way of emphasizing the responsibility of the disciples to give good example to the world around them, especially in their living out of the new doctrine of Christ's kingdom. A lamp is not lit so that its light may be wasted under a bed or a jar. So, too, the city located in a high position has an eminence that makes it very conspicuous. Accordingly, the prominent light and the prominent city—in other words, the disciples—have an example in their lives which they are to pass on to others.

THE LAMP OF THE BODY

Mt. 6:22–23

"The lamp of thy body is thine eye. If, therefore, thine eye is sound, thy whole body shall be illuminated; but if thine eye is blind, thy whole body shall be in darkness."

Lk. 11:34–36

"Thine eye is the lamp of thy body. When thine eye is sound, thy whole body will be illuminated; but when it is sightless, then thy whole body is in darkness. See to it, therefore, that the light that is in thee be not darkness. If, then, thy whole body is illuminated, having no dark part, it will be entirely illuminated, as when the lamp with its bright shining gives thee light."

The meaning here is that just as the eye, like a lamp, guides the body properly, so should the sound mind (the "heart") direct one's life with proper singleness of purpose. This agrees with Jesus' words in the preceding verse of Matthew (6:21) concerning true treasure, "Where thy treasure is, there will thy heart be also."

THE OPPONENT ON THE WAY

Mt. 5:25–26

"Make friends with thine opponent quickly, even while thou art with him on the way; lest thine opponent deliver thee to the judge, and the judge commit thee to the charge of the officer, and thou be thrown into prison. Indeed, I tell thee thou shalt by no means come out of it till thou has repaid the last cent."

Lk. 12:58–59

"While any of you are accompanying an opponent to the magistrate, you have to take pains on the way to effect a release from him; lest he drag you before the judge, and the judge commit you to the officer, and the officer throw you into prison. I tell you, you shall by no means come out of it till you have paid the very last mite."

In the context of both Matthew and Luke, Jesus has warned His listeners of their accountability to God. In Matthew, there is question of uncharitable words and hatred; in Luke, it is a matter of seeing the propinquity of God's judgment. Therefore, with spiritual prudence you should "make friends with thine opponent quickly, even while thou art with him on the way." In terms of the lesson of this condensed parable, we should settle our spiritual accounts with God long before He comes to demand the final accounting. On that day when we are judged, if we are unprepared, it will be as if "thine opponent deliver thee to the judge, and the judge commit thee to the charge of the officer, and thou be thrown into prison. Indeed, I tell thee thou shalt by no means come out of it till thou hast repaid the last cent." Actually, like the man who compromises with his opponent so as to be free from the drastic court action, so should we come to terms with God by repentant adjustment of our life to His law.

PEARLS BEFORE SWINE

Mt. 7:6
"Do not give what is holy to dogs, nor throw your pearls before swine, lest they trample them under their feet, and turning upon you, tear you."

All commentators on this parable are agreed that the general meaning of the admonition is a warning not to profane sacred things. It would mean that the disciples were not to transmit the sacred doctrines of Christ's kingdom to those who were indifferent about them. The first carelessness of the hearers might then turn to malevolence, and like swine disappointed in finding precious pearls instead of edible food they would turn upon the benefactors who have given them spiritual food far too ethereal for their earthbound tastes to appreciate.

Partly because of the parallelism that should exist in an expression of thought so Semitic as this, many scholars look with favor on a theory that reconstructs the meaning of the word "holy." In Aramaic this word so closely resembles "rings" (of gold) that it may have been translated by mistake into its present form. The original words of Jesus would then read, "Do not give your gold rings to dogs, nor throw your pearl necklaces before swine," meaning as before, "These animals will fail to appreciate the value of your gifts, and in their spite will turn on you and rend you limb from limb."

AS THE TREE, SO THE FRUIT

Mt. 7:16–20
"Do people gather grapes from thorn-bushes or figs from thistles? Thus, every good tree produces good fruit, but the decayed tree produces bad fruit. A good tree cannot produce bad fruit, nor can a decayed tree produce good fruit. Every tree not producing good fruit is cut down and thrown on the fire. Therefore, by their fruits you will recognize them."

Mt. 12:33
"Either admit that the tree is good and its fruit good, or else show that the tree is rotting and its fruit decayed; for the tree is known by its fruit."

Lk. 6:43–45
"For there is no good tree that produces bad fruit, nor again a decayed tree that produces good fruit; for every tree is known by its own fruit. For people do not gather figs from thorn-bushes, nor pluck a bunch of grapes from a bramble-bush. The good man produces good out of the good treasure of his heart; and the bad man produces evil out of his evil treasure; for out of the abundance of the heart his mouth speaks."

Jesus evidently used the comparison of trees and their fruits on more than one occasion, as appears to be the case with His words in Matthew 7 and Matthew 12. The idea, however, is the same in both cases: Good effects can come only from a good cause. Jesus is talking not so much of the personal lives of false teachers as of their doctrine. Hence, His warning seems to extend much further than the immediate dangers in His time from the doctrine of the Pharisees.

Sometimes it has been alleged that this condensed parable is not using a comparison that is true to fact. A healthy tree often enough produces a certain percentage of rotten fruit in addition to its normal good yield. Such an objection, however, fails to note the comparison as Jesus made it. He Himself asked whether "people gather grapes from thorn-bushes or figs from thistles." The question, therefore, concerns the *kind* of fruit, and not so much the *amount* of healthy fruit from a particular tree.

None the less, the parable holds true as a wider rule, provided it is not illogically pushed to an unintended extreme. Normally, healthy trees provide healthy fruit, and normally, too, healthy fruit cannot grow on a poor tree. The "goodness" and "badness" of the trees in this parable is evidently related to the goodness and evil in the lives of the teachers Jesus discusses. All error must have at least a grain of truth in itself in order to live. These teachers are to be carefully scrutinized, and the effects of their doctrine will reveal its soundness. One is reminded of our modern proverb in this respect, "Look for the devil's tail!" In other words, see whether good is consistently done or whether evil gradually and insidiously is making an otherwise unnoticed entry.

THE CLIENTS OF THE PHYSICIAN

Mt. 9:12–13

"The healthy have no need of a physician, but the sick have. Now go and learn what this means: 'I desire mercy, and not sacrifice'; for I have not come to call righteous people, but sinners."

Mk. 2:17

"The healthy have no need of a physician, but the sick have. I did not come to call righteous people, but sinners."

Lk. 5:31–32

"The healthy have no need of a physician, but the sick have. I have not come to call righteous people, but sinners, to repentance."

The Pharisees and scribes were scandalized at the fact that Jesus ate in the company of publicans and sinners. They reproached the disciples for the conduct of their master. When Jesus heard of this, He reminded His listeners that He as the divine physician had come for the sake of sinners, for those who were morally ill. This did not mean that He was uninterested in those leading good lives, but that the self-righteous and spiritually proud would not be the recipients of His message until they, too, would humble themselves and acknowledge their need for God's mercy on their sinfulness. He quoted in this respect the words of Osee 6:6, "I desire mercy, and not sacrifice."

THE FRIENDS OF THE BRIDEGROOM

Mt. 9:14–15

Then the disciples of John approached Him, asking, "Why is is that, while we and the Pharisees fast often, Thy disciples do not fast?" "Can the groomsmen be mournful," Jesus answered them, "as long as the bridegroom is with them?"

Mk. 2:18–20

Both the disciples of John and the disciples of the Pharisees were fasting; and they came and asked Him, "Why is it that, while the disciples of John and of the Pharisees fast, Thy disciples do not fast?" "Can the groomsmen fast," Jesus answered them, "while the bridegroom is with them? As long as they have the bridegroom with them they cannot fast."

Lk. 5:33–35

"Why is it," they then asked Him, "that, while the disciples of John, and those of the Pharisees as well, fast frequently and repeat prayers, Thine eat and drink?" "Can you compel the groomsmen to fast," Jesus replied to them, "while the bridegroom is with them? But other days are coming—and when the bridegroom shall be taken away from them, then they will fast in those days."

The meaning of this condensed parable has been obscured by the older English translations that speak of the "children of the bridegroom." This meaning stemmed from the ancient Hebrew idiom which should appear in modern English as "friends of the bridegroom" or simply "wedding guests."

The conduct of Jesus in not observing all the fasts so strictly enjoined by the Pharisees had been the source of complaint on their part, and had been a difficulty likewise for the disciples of John the Baptist. Accordingly, the question was put to Jesus why

His followers did not fast like the followers of the Baptist. Jesus' answer, we must note, does not disparage the custom of fasting. In fact, He says that in later days His disciples will truly mourn and fast—a veiled reference to His passion and death. For the present, however, He, the bridegroom, is with them. For that reason it would ill befit His disciples to show signs of mourning. They are like those guests at the wedding whose duty it is to amuse the groom and the bride, certainly, then, to be joyful.

THE OLD AND THE NEW

Mt. 9:16–17

"No one inserts a patch of new cloth into an old garment; for the insertion would tear away a portion from the garment, and a worse rent would be made. Nor do men put new wine into old wine skins; for if they did, the skins would burst, and the wine be spilled, and the skins destroyed."

Mk. 2:21–22

"No one sews a patch of new cloth on an old garment; if he did, the new filling would tear away from the old stuff, and a worse rent would be made. And no one puts new wine into old wine-skins; if he did, the wine would burst the skins, and the wine would be spilled, and the skins destroyed. On the contrary, new wine must be put into fresh wine-skins."

Lk. 5:36–39

"No one inserts in an old garment a patch he has torn from a new garment; if he did, not only would he tear the new garment, but the patch taken from the new would not harmonize with the old. And no one puts new wine into old wine-skins; if he did, the new wine would burst the skins, and itself would be spilled and the skins destroyed. On the contrary, new wine must be put into fresh wine-skins. And nobody drinking old wine at once desires new; for he says, 'The old is better.' "

At this point the synoptic gospels present three brief parables to show that the old and the new cannot be mixed. Luke adds a fourth saying of Jesus to round out the lesson even more.

The examples are taken from everyday experience which Jesus' hearers would readily understand. One does not sew unshrunk new cloth into old cloth as a patch, for the strong and shrinking patch will merely rip the old cloth and make the rent larger. Similarly, one does not put new, fermenting wine into old wine-skins, but new wine must be put into fresh wineskins. Otherwise, the skins will burst, weakened as they are from previous fermentation within them and from repeated handling. Both the new wine and the old bottles in such a case will be lost. We must remember that these "bottles" of the times of Jesus were goatskins sewed together, containers that were far different from the strong glass bottles of our own day.

The exact meaning of these parables is open to discussion, but the general meaning is certain. Jesus is teaching the radical newness (that is, "new from the roots") of the doctrine of the kingdom. The Mosaic law truly came from God, and fulfilled its purpose for as long as it was to last. None the less, it was now superseded by the Christian new covenant between God and man. Jesus delicately implies that the two covenants are so disparate that while the second builds on the first, they cannot be mixed without destroying the good that exists in both of them. One cannot be a Christian and a Jew at the same time. The new must replace the old completely, and thus only can it fulfill the promises and the preparation of the old.

The closing comment added in Luke continues the simile of

old and new wine, but in a different manner. "Nobody drinking old wine at once desires new, for he says, 'The old is better.'" This seems to be a sympathetic reassurance of Jesus that He understands the difficulties of the faithful Jew in giving up the law which Israel had held for so long as the law of God. "Nobody *at once* desires the new." Is this not a hint of the educative process that will be necessary when the disciples eventually see the need for the complete break from Judaism? Even in their case, they had to learn the lesson gradually.

THE GREAT HARVEST

Mt. 9:37–38
"The harvest is plentiful, but the laborers are few. Pray, there-fore, the Master of the harvest to send out laborers into His harvest."

Lk. 10:2
"The harvest is plentiful, but the laborers are few. Pray there-fore the Master of the harvest to send out laborers into His harvest."

This compressed parable follows the description of Jesus' com-passion for the multitudes whom He saw as sheep that have no shepherd. He mentioned the idea a second time when He com-missioned the seventy disciples to preach His gospel throughout the land. "The harvest is plentiful, but the laborers are few. Pray, therefore, the Master of the harvest to send out laborers into His harvest."

The harvest evidently represents souls who are to be brought to the knowledge of Christ; the laborers are the preachers of

Christ's word; the Master is God the Father. The justifiable conclusion to be drawn from Jesus' comparison is that much good can be done if only the human instruments are available. Moreover, prayer to God works wonders in winning the graces necessary for such an apostolic expansion.

Certain other conclusions, however, are positively excluded. Such would be the opinion that the "harvest" here represents the end of the world instead of membership in the Church of Christ in this life. Again, may not one infer an answer in either direction as to the great mystery of the number of the saved? The answer is a definite "no." But if the harvest is so plentiful, does this not mean that most souls are to be saved? Or in the opposite direction, if the laborers are so few, does this not mean that most souls will be lost because the gospel has not been preached to them? The reply in each case must always be, "We do not know." From the context of this little parable Jesus did not intend to teach in any way the solution to the question He elsewhere refused to answer concerning the number of the saved. The certain fact remaining for us is the duty to save our own souls, the one fact over which we have absolute control.

Most striking in the parable is the use of the "law of solidarity." In other words the human race goes to God not only as individuals but also as a group, a unit. Hence, our prayers are necessary in order to obtain apostolic success for the Church. One may reasonably wonder whether the failure of Christianity to convert all mankind after these nineteen centuries of opportunity is to be attributed to the lack of prayer for such success.

The answer is neither simple nor single. On the one hand, we recall that Jesus Himself, He who was God almighty possessing human nature, failed miserably as far as the extent of His apostolate was concerned. If Jesus Himself, incarnate holiness and wisdom, failed thus, can we blame men for having failed after Him, too? Jesus prayed for laborers in the harvest, with an efficacy of prayer no human being can possess. The powerful prayers of

Mary and Joseph were certainly joined to His, and yet the failure of Calvary has been extended into every century after Jesus. Are we not in the midst of the mystery of the divine toleration of evil in the world, as well as the relationship of God's grace and man's free will?

From another viewpoint we must consider that the Church of Christ has suffered not only because of persecution by iniquitous men from outside it and not only because of the treachery of new Judases within its bosom. At least equally responsible for its difficulties have been factors beyond its control: ignorance, only too often honest and sincere but still most muddled; cataclysms of nature, like plagues and earthquakes and fire; economic and social pressures, like barbarian invasions, greed for national power and independent sovereignty, terrible wars; and inventions and cultural advances, like the printing press, world-wide travel, and the impact of electronics. All these have vitally contributed to an advance or a check of the Church's power to spread its message.

For all these reasons we cannot come to a final conclusion concerning the harvest in our own day, as to why it could be still so plentiful and why the laborers are still so few. Our decision today must be the same that issued from the mouth of Jesus centuries ago: "Pray the Master of the harvest to send out laborers into His harvest." Provided we have done and are doing our part, we must place the problem into the hands of God, and with that rest content, conformed to what His will permits.

AS TO THE SUPERIOR, SO TO THE SUBJECT

Mt. 10:24–25

"A disciple is not above his master, nor a slave above his lord. It is enough for the disciple to be like his master, and the slave, like his lord."

Jn. 13:16

"A slave is not greater than his master, nor is a messenger greater than he who has sent him."

Jn. 15:20

"Remember what I said to you before, 'A slave is not greater than his master.' "

Three short comparisons appear in these words of Jesus, all of which are based on an *a fortiori* reasoning. Because a disciple is less than his teacher and a slave is less than his master, we cannot be surprised when the enemies of the superior treat the subject in the same way they treated his lord. If the master of the household has been insulted with the term "Beelzebul" (prince of evil), by a stronger line of reasoning the members of the household will be assailed even more than he.

But "do not fear them, for there is nothing concealed that shall not be revealed, nor secret that shall not become known." In other words, the secret plottings of such enemies will eventually be exposed by God and will be punished for justice' sake.

THE DIVIDED KINGDOM

Mt. 12:25-28

"Every kingdom divided against itself is brought to ruin; and no city or family divided against itself shall endure. So if Satan casts out Satan, he is divided against himself; how then shall his kingdom endure? And if I cast out demons by the agency of Beelzebul, by whose agency do your own disciples cast them out?

They, therefore, shall be your judges! But if I by the spirit of God cast out demons, then the Kingdom of God has overtaken you!"

Mk. 3:23–27

"How can Satan expel Satan? And if a kingdom is divided against itself, that kingdom cannot endure. And if a family is divided against itself, that family cannot endure. So if Satan has rebelled against himself, he is divided, and cannot endure, but has reached his end. However, nobody can enter the dwelling of the strong one and plunder his property unless he first binds the strong one; and then he will plunder his dwelling."

Lk. 11:17–18

"Any kingdom divided against itself shall be brought to ruin, and house upon house shall fall. If, then, Satan, also is divided against himself, how shall his kingdom endure?—since you assert that I cast out demons by the agency of Beelzebul."

Jesus again was accused by the Pharisees as an agent of Beelzebul, the prince of demons, because He was casting out devils. This simple parable served to show how unreasonable such a statement had to be: A kingdom, city, or family divided against itself with internal strife cannot endure for long. If Satan himself casts out Satan, would this not indicate he was undermining his own kingdom? We might understand that he would act apparently against himself on one or two occasions in order to achieve his nefarious ends; but to do so consistently would go counter to even his malevolent (though highly gifted and angelic) intelligence. (Incidentally, the word "satan" means "adversary" or "opponent," and thus came to be applied to the devil, the chief of the fallen angels, and our opponent par excellence.) Thus, when Jesus freed people of their possession by evil spirits, He evidently did so by His own divine power and not by the power of the evil one.

The mention of diabolical possession in the gospels calls for some explanation here. The phenomenon has been scientifically witnessed in lands and centuries far removed from the Palestine of Jesus, and cannot be dismissed as a fantasy or as a mistaken diagnosis of what should objectively be termed epilepsy or grave mental disturbance.

Two elements are found in possession: the presence of the devil and perhaps devils in the body of the possessed, and the quasi-dominion which the devil exerts over the body and, to some extent, the soul. The free will of the possessed person is left intact.

To quote Father Tanquerey's analysis, "We can distinguish two distinct states in possessed persons: the crisis, and the period of calm. The crisis is like a violent attack in which the devil manifests his tyrannical sway by imparting to the body a feverish agitation which finds expression in contortions, outbursts of fury, and impious and blasphemous utterances. Thereupon, the victims seem to lose all sense of what takes place within them, and they retain no memory of what they say or do, or rather, of what the devil does through them. It is only at the beginning of the crisis that they are aware of the invasion of the evil one, and after that they apparently lose consciousness." (Tanquerey, *The Spiritual Life*, page 72.)

It is worth noting once again that a similarity exists between epileptic convulsions, certain manic and hysteric states, and the external manifestations of diabolical possession. None the less, definite signs also exist which distinguish the one from the other. The chief indication of the diabolic presence lies in a manifestation of a suprahuman intelligence concerning things religious. Such knowledge could be discerned by means of no natural channel of telepathy or clairvoyance, whether in a state of good health or as a result of abnormal mental conditions. The Church

144

strictly enjoins the greatest caution in this field lest exorcisms be performed rashly in cases where only disease exists, or lest in genuine possessions the devil be permitted to wreak even greater harm.

THE DOMINION OF DEMONS

Mt. 12:43-45

"When the foul spirit has gone out of a man, he wanders about in waterless places in search of rest, but finds none. Then he says, 'I will return to my dwelling from which I came'; and on arriving he finds it unoccupied, swept and adorned. Then he goes and brings with him seven other spirits more wicked than himself, and they enter and dwell there; and the final condition of that man becomes worse than the first. So, too, shall it be with this wicked generation."

Lk. 11:24-26

"When the foul spirit has gone out from the man, he wanders about in waterless places in search of rest; and finding none he says, 'I will return to my dwelling whence I came out.' And on arriving he finds it swept and adorned. Then he goes and brings with him seven other spirits more wicked than himself, and they enter and dwell there; and the final condition of that man becomes worse than the first."

The preceding comments on diabolical possession can serve again to introduce the short parable of Jesus concerning the "foul spirit" that "has gone out of a man, wanders about in waterless places in search of rest, but finds none." The devil then returns to the soul delivered from his influence and brings with him "seven other spirits" (a typical round number) more wicked than himself. "The final condition of that man becomes worse than the first. So, too, it shall be with this wicked generation."

The fact of diabolical possession in itself is already so mysterious to our understanding that a parable of this sort is obscure from the very nature of its subject, let alone its lesson. That lesson, however, was not lost on hearers who saw in their experience more than enough instances of possession to convince them of its reality. Applied to the Jews, it would mean that if leaders of the people in their culpability refused the message of Jesus, they would be left, as it were, spiritually untenanted. Their indifference to God's will would be an invitation to Satan to take them over, and in such a case their lot would be spiritually far worse than it had been before God first called the nation to Himself at the time of Abraham.

Applied to the people in general of Christ's time, the little parable warns that after Jesus' words drive away the demonic influence, serious efforts must be put forth in order to prevent the devil's return in an attempted stronger counterattack. If the devil succeeds with his renewed and increased campaign, the spiritual state of these people will now be worse than it was before.

TRUE DEFILEMENT; THE UPROOTED PLANT; BLIND GUIDES

Mt. 15:10–20

"Listen and understand! Not that which goes into the mouth profanes a man; but what comes out of the mouth does profane a man." Then His disciples approached and said to Him, "Dost

Thou know that the Pharisees were scandalized at hearing this remark?" But He said in reply, "Every plant which My heavenly Father has not planted shall be uprooted. Let them alone; they are blind guides of the blind; and if the blind guides the blind, both will fall into the pit." Peter, replying, said to Him, "Explain this parable to us." "Are you, too," He answered, "even yet without comprehension? Do you not perceive that everything that goes into the mouth makes its way into the bowels and is evacuated? But the things that come out of the mouth proceed from the heart, and they profane a man. For out of the heart proceed wicked thoughts, murders, adulteries, fornications, thefts, false testimonies, blasphemies; these are what profane a man. But to eat with unwashed hands does not profane a man."

Mk. 7:15–23

"Listen to Me, all of you, and understand. There is nothing outside a man which by entering him can profane him; but the things which proceed from a man, these are what profane a man."

Now, when He had gone into the house from the crowd, His disciples questioned Him about this obscure saying. "Are you, too," He said to them, "so dull of comprehension? Do you not understand that nothing that enters a man from without can profane him, since it does not enter his heart, but his bowels, and is evacuated?" Thus pronouncing all food clean, He added, "It is what proceeds from a man that profanes a man. For from within, from the heart of men, proceed wicked thoughts, fornications, thefts, murders, adulteries, avarice, villainies, deceit, profligacy, an evil eye, blasphemy, slander, levity. All these evils proceed from within, and profane a man."

Lk. 6:39

"Can the blind guide the blind? Will they not both fall into a pit?"

These three short parables that occur in the first half of Matthew's fifteenth chapter are easily understood once we see them in their context. The Pharisees had challenged Jesus for the habits of His disciples in neglecting the customary washing of hands which pharisaic tradition so inflexibly enjoined. Jesus replied by quoting from the scriptures, particularly Isaiah, to show the hypocrisy of having "annulled the word of God for the sake of your tradition." In order to counteract this exaggerated attention to such rituals, He added, "Not that which goes into the mouth profanes a man; but that which comes out of the mouth profanes a man."

We should note carefully that Jesus is not condemning rite and ritual and ceremony as such. It is only and always the *exaggeration* He has in mind, where the letter of the law has completely lost its connection with the spirit. To put this in different wording, Jesus condemns the situation where religious observance decays into external formalism without the sincere intention of pleasing God, the intention that vivifies all our religious service.

But the Pharisees openly professed their scandal at Jesus' equally open denunciation of what was now meaningless tradition. Therefore, with regard to them, Jesus remarked, "Every plant which My heavenly Father has not planted shall be uprooted." This points out that if the spirit of the Pharisees is divorced from the spirit of genuine submission to God, they will be removed from the scene and lose all their power. The reference does not seem here to be to the individuals as such, but rather to the sect. God will disavow their vain observance.

To make this point even stronger, Jesus adapted a current proverb to His purpose. The Pharisees in their spiritual obstinacy were blind guides. Hence, all who followed them were equally blind. Such stubbornness could result only in the utter destruction of both leaders and led.

We are confused at this point to read that "Peter, *replying*, said to Him . . ." There was actually no question of answering any question of Jesus; Matthew has faithfully kept the Aramaic idiom which would mean in modern English that Peter "spoke up."

At any rate, Peter asked in the name of the disciples precisely what the first parable about true profanation meant, for he and the rest still did not understand its application. How could anything profane a man if it came out of his mouth? Jesus made His point at once. Food that enters one's mouth is good in itself, a creation of God, that undergoes the ordinary processes of digestion and elimination. But what "comes from the mouth" actually "proceeds from the heart." Accordingly, not only "false testimonies and blasphemies" are the things that profane a man, but the "wicked thoughts, murders, adulteries, fornications, and thefts." Jesus closed the parable with a résumé, "But to eat with unwashed hands does not profane a man."

CRUMBS FOR THE DOGS

Mt. 15:26–27

"It is not fair to take the children's bread, and throw it to the dogs." "True, Lord," she said, "yet even the dogs feed on the crumbs that fall from their masters' table."

Mk. 7:27–28

"Allow the children to be fed first; for it is not fair to take the children's bread and throw it to the dogs." "True, Lord," she said to Him in reply, "yet even the dogs under the table eat of the children's crumbs."

After the denunciation of the empty rites of washing, Jesus went into the pagan districts farther north. Here occurred one of the most charming events of Christ's public life. The repartee that was exchanged between Him and a woman of the area shows how kind were His actions and how thoughtful were His words even though they might appear harsh out of context. The real reason was evidently Jesus' desire to perfect the woman's faith.

Persistently, she asked Jesus to cure her daughter, who was possessed by a devil. Jesus answered not a word, but His conduct was such that He made it apparent He was not repulsing her. When her persistence irritated the disciples, they approached Jesus to have her sent away and thus give them some respite. At the same time they were probably wondering at an apparent rude silence from one who was the soul of kindness. But Jesus' mode of acting showed its reasonableness without delay.

In the original plan of God, He was to restrict Himself to the Jews, the Chosen People, and the working of a miracle of exorcism here in gentile country would have unduly extended His apostolate. None the less, the woman's love was to do violence, as it were, to the original scheme. Her repeated prayer, "Lord, do help me!" moves our hearts even across the nineteen centuries that separate us from its first utterance. How the human heart of Jesus must have been moved!

Still making a point of preference for the Jews, He quoted the proverb, "It is not fair to take the children's bread and throw it to the dogs." The "children" would be the Jewish nation, chosen by God as the means to bring salvation to the rest of the world after first accepting it themselves. The "dogs" would represent the gentiles.

Yet we are not to forget the point of comparison in the parable. Jesus did not call the Jews children, nor the gentiles dogs; and the proverb He cited has a fuller implication. The father of the house saves food for his children, and he will not sacrifice his children's welfare for the *little* dogs—pets, in other words—who

150

scamper around the table. This was, of course, the opening for the pagan woman. She respectfully but still persistently reminded the dear Lord Himself that these same pets were given the scraps and crumbs which the children did not want nor need. In other words she recognized the freedom of God in distributing His gifts as He willed, and she would be grateful for *any* gift He gave her, even the smallest.

So it was that Jesus exclaimed, "O woman, great is thy faith! Be it done to thee as thou wilt." Her daughter was freed from the diabolic possession at the moment.

THE LAST PLACE AT THE SUPPER

Lk. 14:7–11

Then, observing how the invited guests were choosing the first places at table, He gave them a lesson, saying to them: "When thou art invited by any one to a wedding-feast, do not recline in the place of honor, lest one more distinguished than thou be invited by him, and the one who invited thee and him come and say to thee, 'Give place to this gentleman'; and then thou begin with shame to take the last place. On the contrary, when thou art invited, go and recline in the last place; so that, when thy host comes, he may say to thee, 'My friend, go up higher.' Thou wilt then be honored in the presence of all thy fellow-guests. For every one who exalts himself shall be humiliated; but he who humbles himself shall be exalted."

This is a very simple parable condemning ostentatious pride, and suggesting proper humility. Jesus had witnessed only too often the maneuvers of invited guests in seeking places of honor at the banquets. He accordingly reminded His listeners that if they usurp a position of honor, they take the risk of being later demoted by the host, who will substitute a more honored guest in their place. On the other hand, if they seek the lower places, they lose nothing and have the chance to gain more. The invitation of their host to "go up higher" will increase their prestige all the more.

To get the local color of this parable, we should remember that the Jews had adopted the Greek custom of reclining at banquets. The table was usually horseshoe shaped. The servants brought food from the inside of the horseshoe. As mentioned earlier, the guests reclined on their left elbows on divans, while they ate with their right hands. This custom, too, the gospels imply when they repeatedly say that Jesus "reclined" with His disciples at table.

COUNTING THE COSTS

Lk. 14:28-33

"For which of you, wishing to build a castle, will not first sit down and calculate the cost, to ascertain whether he has enough to complete it? lest, having laid a foundation, and not being able to finish, all the beholders should begin to ridicule him, saying 'This man began to build, and was unable to finish!' Or what king, as he goes to encounter another king in war, will not first sit down and deliberate whether he is able with ten thousand men to meet the one who is advancing against him with twenty thousand. And if he is not, he will, while the other is still at a distance, send an embassy to sue for conditions of peace. So therefore not one of you can be My disciple who does not renounce all that he has."

Two condensed parables are mentioned here by Jesus. Any man having the wish to build an elaborate structure such as a castle will not begin his undertaking until he is reasonably sure that he can complete it. So, too, no king will go into a war when he knows that the forces opposing his men are twice as strong.

The lesson Jesus draws refers to the conditions for being His disciple. There seems to be no question here of following Jesus in a more perfect way by manner of counsel. The issue at stake is the acceptance of Jesus' message, the membership in His kingdom and in His church. More paradox exists in these two brief comparisons, however, than appears at first sight. In worldly affairs money (for the building) and power (for the conquest) are necessary. But in the spiritual kingdom of Jesus the detachment from money and power is an essential for entrance.

The follower of Christ must realize, then, that the law of Jesus demands a renunciation of money, family ties, even one's own life. Jesus certainly taught this lesson again and again in other parts of His preaching. Here it is to be understood as always: The renunciation Jesus asks must be that of spiritual detachment, ready to give up any creature, be it person or thing or circumstance of one's life, if it threatens to stand in the way of following Jesus. In line with sound reason, of course, we add the interpretation of all spiritual masters that Jesus does not condemn the use of created things and persons which lead us to Him. It is only and always this question of inordinate attachment that requires the mortification mentioned here.

THE EXEMPTION OF THE SON OF THE KING

Mt. 17:24–25

When they came to Capharnaum, the collectors of the half-shekel tax came to Peter and asked him, "Does not your Master pay the half-shekel?" "Yes," said he. And when he came into the house Jesus anticipated him, saying, "What is thy opinion, Simon? From whom do earthly kings take tolls or taxes? from their own sons or from other people?" And when he said, "From other people," Jesus said to him, "Then the sons are free."

This brief parable is part of the episode concerning Jesus' payment of the temple tax. The tax amounted to half a shekel or two denarii, the ordinary pay for two days' labor.

When Jesus returned to Capharnaum, the collectors approached Peter and asked rather diffidently whether his master was subject to this taxation. Peter impulsively answered, "Yes" in the name of Jesus. Since the priests of the temple were exempt, it is possible that these collectors—local representatives as they were—wondered whether Jesus' dignity as a teacher made Him exempt, too. But on entering his house, Peter found that Jesus was aware of the conversation either by supernatural knowledge or by having overheard what was said.

Then Jesus asked Peter, "From whom do earthly kings take toll or taxes? From their own sons or from other people?" The only logical answer was, of course, "From other people," since the taxes were for the support of the king's household. Jesus concluded, "Then the sons are free." Implicitly, He made it clear that He was free, too, and as far as strict justice was concerned Jesus was exempt from paying this religious tax because He was the natural son of the "king"—in this case God Himself.

However, lest scandal be given to those who did not understand His true dignity, Jesus sent Peter to the Lake of Gennesaret, there to find a fish which would have a shekel in its mouth, the amount of the tax for Jesus and Peter. This event seems certainly miraculous, particularly in the knowledge required that the *first* fish Peter would catch on his hook would be carrying the shekel.

As for lessons to be drawn from this parable, Jesus taught that He was exempt by strict right from human law. He included Peter with Himself in the miraculous payment of the tax, but it does not seem that we are justified in saying that Peter, like Jesus, was also exempt as Jesus was. The point can be argued both ways.

The same doubt, however, does not extend to an application of the argument to all future generations of clergymen, as if Jesus were teaching that they are not subject to taxation. The reasons are clear. The temple tax had been a religious much more than a civil tax; and the parable refers to Jesus, who alone is the son of the king by nature. It is doubtful, therefore, whether the phrase "children of the king's household" is to be understood in the plural, to others beyond Jesus, especially to those in generations after Him.

THE WATCHFUL SERVANTS

Mk. 13:33-37

"It is as when a man, traveling abroad, on leaving his house gave authority to his servants—to each one his own task—and commanded the porter to watch. Watch, therefore—for you know not when the Master of the house will come, whether in the evening or at midnight or at cockcrow or in the morning—lest coming suddenly He find you sleeping. But what I say to you, I say to all —Watch!"

"Let your loins be girded and your lamps burning, and you yourselves like men waiting for their master when he returns from the wedding; so that when he comes and knocks they may at once open to him. Happy are those servants whom their master, when he comes, shall find watching. Indeed I tell you that he will gird himself, and make them recline at table, and go about and serve them. And if he comes in the second watch, and if he comes in the third watch, and finds them thus, happy are those servants!"

A favorite theme of Jesus in His parables is the need to be vigilant, to be spiritually ready for the day when God's call comes whether on the day of death or on the Last Day itself. The two present passages of Mark and Luke present apparently a double use of the idea, each on a different occasion and amid different circumstances.

In Mark's account, Jesus' admonition follows the so-called eschatological discourse, the prophecy of the fall of Jerusalem and of the end of the world. We have already commented earlier on this dire and mysterious prediction of Jesus (see page 58). Suffice it to repeat here that two distinct events are mentioned in the prophecy. The one, the fall of Jerusalem, will happen before "this generation pass away"; the other, the end of the world, is a secret known only to God the Father in the sense that Jesus in His messianic mission was not to impart it. To illustrate this fact that "of that day or that hour no one knows, not even the angels in heaven—not even the Son—none but the Father," Jesus uses the example of servants who await the return of their master from a far country. He may suddenly return at evening, midnight, early morning, or dawn. Woe to them if he finds them sleeping instead of tending to the duty he has assigned them!

The cognate parable which Luke recounts returns to the familiar theme of the wedding feast. In this case, however, the servants await the return of their master from the night celebration. Their loins are to be girt, that is, their ankle-length gowns are to be tucked up for facility in walking. Their lamps, too, are to be burning, all in readiness for the master.

With the liberty of the typical Hebrew parable, the story now leaves historical reality and merges into its lesson. The master "will gird himself and make them recline at table, and go about and serve them." The fact is that no master would thus reward his slaves for having merely done their duty. Especially would he avoid the menial task of waiting on them at table.

But the master is evidently Jesus Himself, who hints at the reward He as God has prepared for His faithful servants. It is interesting to see that Mark has mentioned the possible times of the master's return in full detail as evening (the first watch of the night, from about 6:00 to 9:00 P.M.), midnight (the second watch, to midnight), cockcrow (to 3:00 A.M.), and morning (evidently the dawn at the end of the fourth watch, about 6:00 A.M.). In Luke the coming of the master is limited to the second or third watch, a much shorter period.

THE THIEF

Mt. 24:42–44

"Watch, therefore, for you know not on what day your Lord is coming. But be sure of this, that if the householder had known in what part of the night the thief was coming, he would have watched, and not have suffered his house to be broken into. Therefore, be you also ready; for at an unexpected moment the Son of Man will come."

"But be sure of this, that if the householder had known at what hour the thief was coming, he would have watched and not have suffered his house to be broken into. Be you also ready; for at an unexpected moment the Son of Man will come."

At first sight it seems most unbecoming for Jesus to compare Himself to a thief. These two parables of the unexpectedness of the thief's entry have therefore been an occasion for misunderstanding.

As always, we must note carefully the points of comparison. The idea is that *just as* the thief breaks into a house when he thinks the householder will not be prepared to guard against him, so *with similar lack of warning* God's call will come to us, whether at the time of our death or at the end of the world.

THE STEWARD

Mt. 24:45–51

"Who, then, is the faithful and prudent servant whom his master has placed over his household to give them their food at the proper time? Happy is that servant whose master on his arrival finds him thus engaged! Indeed, I tell you that he will place him over all his possessions. But if that wicked servant says in his heart, 'My master delays his coming,' and begins to beat his fellow-servants, and eat and drink with the drunkards, the master of that servant will come on a day when he is not expecting him, and at a moment that he is not aware of, and will severely scourge him, and assign him his place with the hypocrites; there shall be the weeping and the grinding of teeth!"

"Who, now, is the faithful and prudent servant, whom his master will place over his domestics to give them their allowance of food at the proper time? Happy is that servant, whose master on his arrival finds him thus engaged! I tell you truly that he will place him over all his possessions. But if that servant says in his heart, 'My master delays his coming,' and begins to beat the menservants and the maids, and to eat and drink and become drunk, the master of that servant will come on a day when he is not expecting him, and at a moment which he is not aware of, and will severely scourge him, and assign him his place with the faithless. And that servant who knew his master's will, and did not prepare for him, nor acted in accordance with his will, shall be flogged with many stripes; but the one who knew not, yet did what deserved blows, shall be flogged with few. And of every one to whom much has been given, much will be required; and of him to whom they have entrusted much, they will demand the more."

Still more parables teach the lesson of vigilance for God's coming. The present two concern the steward who is put in charge of other domestics of the house. According to Matthew, the faithful steward will be rewarded, but if he becomes wicked and in his drunkenness maltreats the servants he will find that his master will come unexpectedly and "will severely scourge him and assign him his place with the hypocrites; there shall be the weeping and the grinding of teeth!"

In adding this stern conclusion Jesus leaves the realm of parable and clearly teaches the impotent rage and despair of the damned, who have become such because they wished it so. This shows that the lesson of the parable deals with retribution after death: rewards for the good, and punishment for the wicked.

Luke adds to this a further note which Jesus inserted when He used the story on some other occasion. Just as the reward will be great, so will retribution be proportioned to the extent of one's misdeeds. If the steward was unfaithful with culpable ignorance, "he shall be flogged with many stripes; but the one who knew not, yet did what deserved blows, shall be flogged with few."

The principle Jesus enunciates is most important to remember if ever we worry about the application of God's providence to the physically and mentally handicapped, or to the unfortunates who have never had the chance to hear the message of Christ's gospel. "Much will be required of every one to whom much has been given; and of him to whom they have entrusted much, they will demand the more." God is always fair. He will demand only what is just from His creatures, taking into account all mitigating circumstances.

THE BODY AND THE EAGLES (VULTURES)

Mt. 24:28

"Wherever the carcass is, there shall the vultures be gathered together."

Lk. 17:37

"Wherever the body is, . . . there too will the vultures be gathered."

Wherever the body is, there will the eagles be gathered. The meaning of this brief parable was readily apparent to any farmer who listened to Jesus. When an animal's carcass was thrown into the field, the eagles or vultures would swoop down upon it at once, to devour what they could before the jackals and hyenas and wolves appeared.

Jesus mentioned the comparison in connection with His prophecy of the fall of Jerusalem and the end of the world. It meant, "Just as the presence of vultures in the air tells you that carrion lies beneath them, so the signs will tell you that the fall of Jerusalem is nigh; be prepared" (see page 58).

THE MYSTERIOUS WIND

Jn. 3:8

"The wind blows where it pleases, and thou hearest its voice; but thou knowest not whence it comes or whither it goes. So it is of every one who is born of the Spirit."

This succinct comparison has no difficulty in itself. The trouble in understanding it results from a translation that puts the Latin *spiritus* into English as "spirit" instead of "wind," its correct rendering.

When Jesus was instructing Nicodemus, He meant that the Holy Spirit works in our souls gently, quietly, yet effectively. His action is like that of the wind, which we do not see but whose action we hear. We do not know its origin nor its destination, but we know its reality.

THE JOY OF MOTHERHOOD

Jn. 16:20–22

"Indeed, indeed, I say to you, that you shall weep and lament, while the world shall rejoice; and you shall be sorrowful, but your sorrow will be turned into joy. A woman when in childbirth has sorrow, because her hour is come; but when she has given birth to the child she no longer remembers the anguish for the joy that a man is born into the world. And so you also for the present have sorrow; but I will see you again, and your heart shall rejoice, and your joy no man can take from you."

This little parable is self-explanatory, but it calls for special mention because it is one more manifestation of the tenderness of the heart of Jesus. We sometimes forget what it means to have a full human temperament, one that is absolutely inflexible when circumstances demand it, and that is equally yielding and compassionate, all in proper time and in proper measure. So, too, the grand words of Jesus' farewell discourse to His apostles are precious literature never surpassed for their sublimity.

UNPROFITABLE SERVANTS

Lk. 17:6–10

"But which of you, having a slave plowing or tending sheep, will say to him on his return from the field, 'Come at once and sit down to dinner'? Wilt thou not rather say to him, 'Get something ready for my dinner; then gird thyself, and wait upon me while I eat and drink, and after this thou shalt eat and drink'? Does he thank that slave for carrying out his orders? I think not. Just so you also, when you have done everything you have been commanded to do, should say, 'We are unprofitable servants! We have but done what it was our duty to do.' "

This parable can be an ever effective antidote against the rise of pride and conceit when we have done our work well. As Jesus told it to the apostles, the master of the house would hardly wine and dine one of his slaves for having plowed the fields or having tended the sheep. The servant had merely done his duty. "Just so you also, when you have done everything you have been commanded to do, should say: 'We are unprofitable servants! We have but done what it was our duty to do.' "

Even if we have performed works of supererogation, far beyond the call of duty, we must still consider ourselves unprofitable servants, for the gifts of God outweigh our return so very far that we can never approach the point of equality. On the other hand, this rule for keeping us humble should not be wrongly applied as if to discourage us. Jesus is equally firm in reminding us that God knows all we do, and will reward us far beyond our strict deserts.

One other possible misinterpretation of this parable concerns the question of gratitude. When Jesus asks, "Does the master thank that slave for carrying out his order? I think not," this cannot and should not be construed as some sort of divine dispensation from the kindness of saying thank you. It is only in the parable that the master will not thank the slave. The oft repeated doctrine of God's rewards shows that the heavenly Master will act far differently.

Jesus Himself indicated how dear to His heart was the virtue of gratitude. In the verses of Luke which follow this parable of the unprofitable servants, we read of the ten lepers whom Jesus cured (17:11–19). Only one of them returned to hear the words of Christ, "Has none been found returning to give glory to God except this alien?" Yes, Jesus wishes us to be grateful.

Epilogue: The Light of the World

It is not accurate to say that Jesus called Himself the light of the world in a few allegorical parables. One should say with more correctness that the whole tenor of the gospel of St. John reminds us that Jesus is the light of all nations, the fountain of truth and knowledge that leads us to God from whom we came. The comparison is so simple and so natural that we take it for granted; but its very simplicity makes it all the more profound and capable of affording material for lifelong meditation.

At the beginning of this book we called attention to the fact that the parables of Jesus were not to be judged according to strict literary norms of comparison. They were, in general, examples taken from everyday life which more or less merged into the lesson Jesus wished to teach. Their partial obscurity helped Him present truths gradually which could not have been offered abruptly and without the preparation which the parables gave their listeners. Then, too, the very elasticity of the parables, allowing application to so many facts, made them bring forward striking conclusions which had been previously taken for granted and left unnoticed.

The one great doctrine of Jesus, the light of this world, was certainly the law of love of God and of man, exemplified and concretized in the proper use of God's creation. As we conclude this book, we wonder whether there is still not one more great "parable"—unrecognized, perhaps, as such—but still having the basic characteristics of a fact from real life, a comparison, and a lesson. It is a parable of charity, too, and we find it in the prayer Jesus taught to His disciples that has been on the lips of generations of the members of Christ ever since.

"Forgive us our trespasses as we forgive those who trespass against us" (Mt. 6: 12). This is not a parable which Jesus told about someone else, as if He had said, "There was a man and there was a woman who were offended by their neighbors, and they forgave them. In the same way as they gave pardon, so will My heavenly Father pardon them." No, this time Jesus puts the parable into our own mouths. We promise in advance that such will be our conduct: to forgive our brothers and sisters in Christ, because we love them in Christ and because we know that *our* faults, too, call for forgiveness on their part. In the same measure that we promise Jesus we shall forgive, in that measure we ask God to forgive us.

And yet, in a sense this is the one prayer which we hope will never be granted by God according to its exact meaning. Even in uttering it, we realize that we must ask God *not* to forgive us precisely as we forgive our debtors, because our measure of forgiveness and our measure of true Christian love of the brethren is still so far removed from what it should be. May God, then, *not* take us at our word in this respect!

But the ideal remains, as Jesus proposed it to us. If we look on His thinking as parabolic with some sort of comparison involved, then we shall mean it thus, "Just as I promise You, my God, that I will forgive those who have injured me, so I beg of You to forgive me. I cannot and do not ask forgiveness in exactly the same measure in which I have given it to others, for there I have failed and know I shall continue to fail. But at least in so far as I *try* to carry out Your law of love, I trust that You in Your generosity will condescend to my weakness and my selfishness, and forgive me, and help me."

Index of Scriptural Quotations and References

Topical Index

banquet, great, 103
  wedding, 107
Beelzebul, 142 ff.
body and eagles (vultures), 160
bridegroom, friends of, 136

castle building, 152
children, capricious, 87
"children of the bridegroom," 136
city on mountain, 129
clients of physician, 135
cloth old and new, 137
cockle, 17
coin, lost, 66
counting costs, 152
crumbs for dogs, 149

darnel seed, 17
debtor, merciless, 89
debtors, two, 34
defilement, true, 146
demons, dominion of, 145
devil (evil one), 15, 18, 142, 145
disciple not above master, 141
Dives and Lazarus, 79
door, narrow, 114

eschatological discourse, 57, 156, 161

fig tree, barren, 53
  budding, 57
fish net, 27
fool, rich, 51
friend, importunate, 46
furnace of fire, 18, 27, 111

gehenna, 82
glutton, rich, 79
gold pieces, 120
gospels, accuracy, 10
  origin, 10
  synoptic, 10
guest without wedding garment, 109
guides, blind, 146

harvest, great, 139
"heaven and earth shall pass away,"
  58
householder, prudent, 30
houses with firm foundations, 32

Joseph, St., 118, 127, 141
judge, godless, 82
judgment day, 19, 20, 27, 54, 57 ff.,
  109, 115, 119, 121, 123, 131, 140,
  156, 159

king going to war, 152
kingdom divided against itself, 142
"kingdom of heaven," meaning, 4 ff.
  parables of, 15, 17, 21, 23, 24, 26, 27,
  28, 30, 57, 89, 92, 99, 103, 109, 115,
  117, 124, 138, 139, 143, 153

laborers in vineyard, 92
lamp of body, 130
  on lampstand, 129
last place at supper, 151
Lazarus, brother of Mary at Bethany,
  41
  Dives and, 80

171

leaven, 23
light of world, Jesus, 164

"mammon of iniquity," 76
manager, shrewd, 72
"many are called but few are chosen,"
112
Mary of Bethany, 34 n., 37 ff.
Magdalen, 34 n., 37 ff.
mother of Jesus, 10, 66, 118, 141
mashal, 2, 62
motherhood, joy of, 161
mustard seed, 21

old and new, cloth and wine-skins,
137
opponent on way, 131

pagan (Canaanite) woman, 150
parables, nature of, 1 ff.
applied senses, 17, 21, 22, 25, 29, 46
64, 95, 117, 119
moral difficulties concerning, 25,
73, 81, 92, 109, 158
pearl, lost, 26
pearls before swine, 132
penitent woman, anonymous, 34 n.,
37 ff.
Pharisee and publican, 84
"physician, cure thyself," 127
plant uprooted, 146
possession, diabolic, 144, 146
prayer, parables of, 48, 49 ff., 82, 85,
127
publican and Pharisee, 84

reprobation, divine, question not
answered in parables, 7 ff., 16,
27, 112, 114, 116, 140

salt, 128

salvation of mankind. *See* "reprobation"
Samaritan, good, 42
seed growing quietly, 28
servants, unprofitable, 162
watchful, 155
shema, 43
shepherd, good, 60
Simon, leper, 38 ff.
Pharisee, 34 ff., 37 ff.
slave of two masters, 77
slaves, unprofitable, 162
son asking for bread, 48
of king exempted, 154
"Son of Man," explained, 19
son, prodigal, 68
sons, two, 97
sower and his seed, 12 ff.
steward, faithful and prudent, 158
unjust, 72
superior, as to subject, 141
swine, pearls and, 132

talents, 120
tares, 17
tenants, wicked, 98
thief, Lord like, 157
treasure found, 24
tree and its fruit, 133
"turn house upside down," 67

vine, Jesus as, 125
virgins, ten, 117

wedding feast, 156
garment, guest without, 109
weeds, 17
wind, mysterious, 161
wine-skins, old and new, 137
"wisdom justified by her children,"
89